Geography
AND THE
New Agenda

Geography
AND THE
New Agenda

Citizenship, PSHE and Sustainable Development in the Primary Curriculum

Keith Grimwade, Elaine Jackson, Alan Reid and Maggie Smith

General Editor: Keith Grimwade

Geographical
Association

Acknowledgements

Thanks are due to the following for permission to reproduce copyright material: The Qualifications and Curriculum Authority (QCA) for the material on pages 20-21 and 36-37 which is taken from the QCA publication *A Scheme of Work for Key Stages 1 and 2 Geography,* published in 1998. Thanks are due to the Eco-Schools Scheme, run by the Tidy Britain Group, that supplied some of the case study material for Chapter 3.

The Authors

Keith Grimwade is General Adviser, Cambridgeshire LEA (Geography).
Elaine Jackson is Primary Adviser for Trafford.
Alan Reid is a lecturer in the Department of Education, University of Bath.
Maggie Smith is a lecturer in the Faculty of Education, University of the West of England.

ISBN 1 899085 84 X
First published 2000
Impression number 10 9 8 7 6 5 4 3 2 1
Year 2003 2002 2001 2000

Published by the Geographical Association, 160 Solly Street, Sheffield S1 4BF. The Geographical Association is a registered charity: no 313129.

The GA would be happy to hear from other potential authors who have ideas for geography books. You may contact the Publications Officer via the GA at the address above. The views expressed in this publication are those of the authors and do not necessarily represent those of the Geographical Association.

Edited by Rose Pipes
Designed by Ledgard Jepson Ltd.
Printed and bound in England by Amadeus Press, Huddersfield

Contents

Photo: Lois Gunby

Introduction

Geography can be creative with Curriculum 2000's 'new agenda', to the benefit of the curriculum as a whole, and it is the aim of this book to support primary teachers and departments with this process. In particular, the book provides support relating to the introduction of the non-statutory framework for PSHE and citizenship, and education for sustainable development. Thus, it both supplements and up-dates the Geographical Association's *Handbook of Primary Geography* which was published in 1998, before completion of the Curriculum 2000 review.

The new programme of study presents a real opportunity for key stages 1 and 2 geography, even though some content has been removed.

- Primary schools must again follow the programme of study in full.
- The importance of geography is clearly defined.
- The role of geographical enquiry is emphasised which will encourage practical, investigative approaches to the teaching of the subject.
- There is greater flexibility in the programme of study, e.g. schools can choose to teach about either rivers or coasts for the 'water in the landscapes' theme.
- Links with the wider curriculum are made, especially with literacy, numeracy, ICT, PSHE and citizenship.
- Geography is given the lead role for 'education for sustainable development' in the curriculum.

Of these opportunities, the most interesting and significant for geography are those which relate to PSHE, citizenship and education for sustainable development. First, they allow geography to demonstrate its relevance to the wider curriculum. Second, in view of the priority given to issues of citizenship and sustainable development on the current political agenda, they have the potential to raise geography's profile on a broader front.

In each chapter in this book, ideas are given for how schools can plan successfully in order to make the most of opportunities: concepts are defined and placed in context; long- and medium-term planning issues are addressed; teaching and learning activities are presented; and suggestions are given for professional development activities.

Addressing each of the dimensions separately helps with an initial understanding but in reality they will be taught together; indeed, PSHE and citizenship are part of the same framework. Undoubtedly, exploiting their links enhances all three: for example, an environmental topic could combine working co-operatively with others (PSHE); realising that living things have needs (citizenship); and planning for the future (education for sustainable development). This approach is one the authors wish to encourage and is evident in the way units of study and teaching activities have been set out (see Figure 1, pages 10-21).

Keith Grimwade   **January 2000**

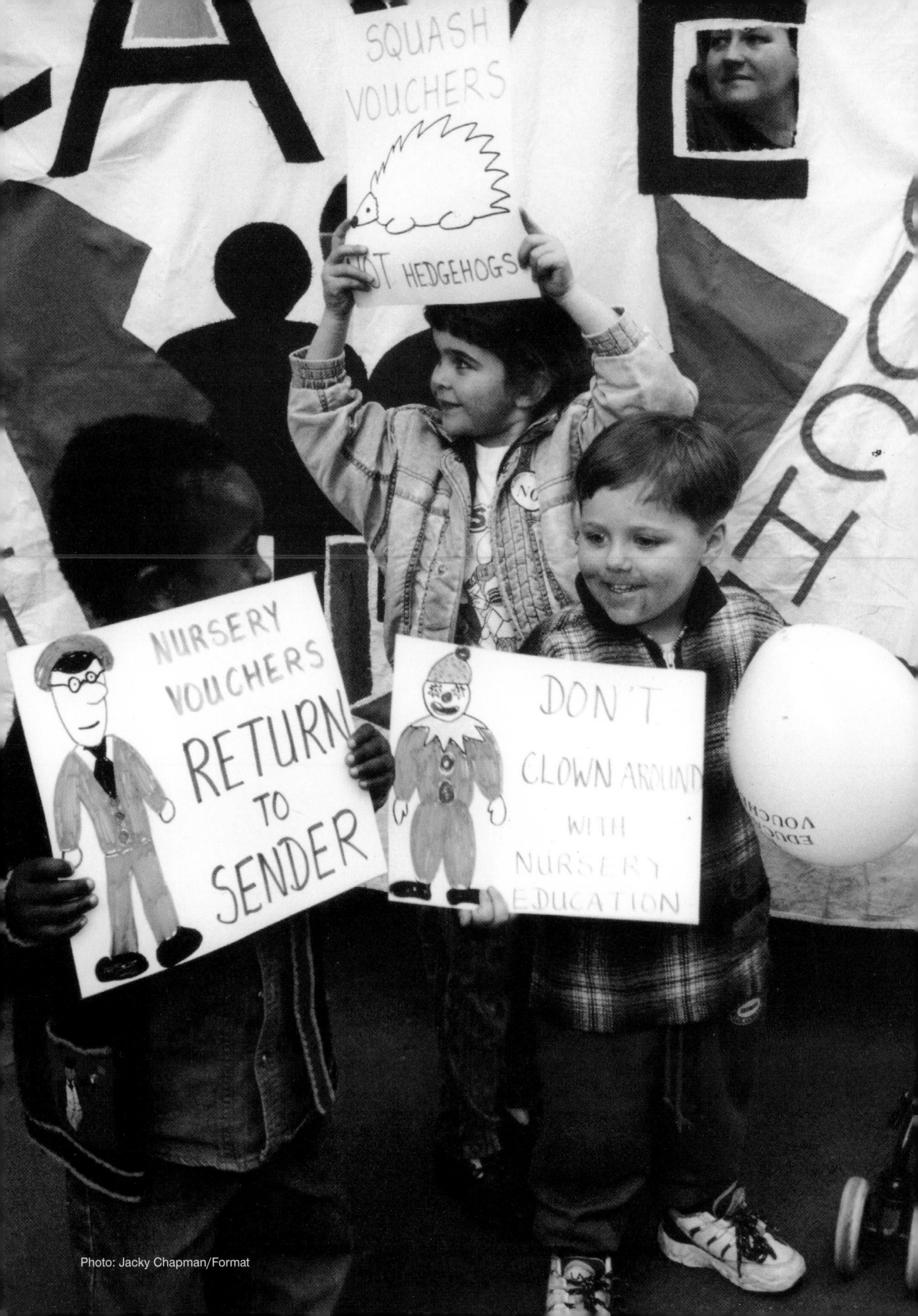

Photo: Jacky Chapman/Format

Citizenship

What is citizenship education?

Many primary schools already have at the core of what they do much that could be described as an education for citizenship. They set out to encourage responsible behaviour in pupils and the importance of ethos, codes of conduct and the individual's role as an effective member of the school community.

However, the teaching of citizenship issues has, even where taught well and effectively, been patchy and lacking in coherence. The experiences offered to children have varied widely. Progression and continuity issues, both within schools and cross-phase, have not really been tackled and as a result there has been no equity in the provision of citizenship education. Where citizenship education has been successful, planned learner outcomes have been identified and shared with all involved, including the pupil and the wider community.

The curriculum for citizenship offers pupils the opportunity to gain the knowledge and understanding of how communities are organised, how there are similarities and differences between individuals, groups and communities and how the needs of individuals are reconciled with those of society. The development of this knowledge and understanding helps the children, both as individuals and as members of their communities, to become aware of issues of fairness and justice, and of their duties, rights and responsibilities as informed, active and responsible citizens in a modern democracy. It enables them to participate in the life of their schools and communities and to learn about the main political and social institutions that affect their lives.

The process of democratic decision making is promoted and the skills of reflective, critical thinking, rational discussion and informed problem solving are developed.

The National Curriculum, Handbook for Primary Teachers in England, Key Stages 1 and 2 states that citizenship helps 'to give pupils the knowledge, skills and understanding they need to lead confident, healthy, independent lives and to become informed, active and responsible citizens' (QCA/DfEE, 1999).

Education for citizenship is essentially about the processes which explore values, and attitudes. It provides real contexts and opportunities to engage the pupils as active participants, and offers them time for reflection and response. Pupils have the opportunity to compare values and beliefs held by themselves and others, to examine evidence and opinions critically, to form conclusions, discuss differences and resolve conflicts. High on the citizenship agenda is the development of attitudes and values which promote self-respect and respect for others, encourage respect for democracy, justice, law and human rights and develop social and moral responsibility.

Citizenship education helps pupils develop the strategies to form effective and fulfilling relationships, which are essential to life and learning – relationships that recognise common humanity and respect the diversity of and differences between people.

Involving pupils as active participants is a very important element of citizenship education.

> 'Tell me and I might hear you, show me and I might see, involve me and I will understand.' (Junior Citizen Award Scheme, Hampshire)

Geography is one of the curriculum areas which has integral links to elements of citizenship education and which can provide a vehicle for enhancing the quality and value of citizenship education delivered in schools. Through primary geography children are encouraged to study places at a range of scales, from local to global, and to explore the interdependence of society, economy and the natural environment. Children are encouraged to study how people are influenced by and affect their environments and to develop a sense of responsibility for personal and group actions. Primary geography provides opportunities for learners to encounter and engage in real issues; issues which may cross a range of scales, from local to global, and which require active participation and personal responses. Children are encouraged to listen carefully to arguments from different viewpoints and to reflect on these points of view.

Primary geography and citizenship education both involve the application of the six key skills – communication, working with others, problem solving and learning, information technology, application of number, and improving own learning and performance – to real issues and concerns. Learning is more meaningful and exciting for children when it involves real-life, real-world issues which have an impact on their own lives and which they feel part of and able to contribute to in ways that make a real difference. Primary geography helps children become aware of the wider world and how that world works economically, socially, culturally, technologically and environmentally. Ideas of fair trade and of sustainability, in all its forms, can easily be woven into the children's geographical studies; indeed, they should be treated as key concepts.

What are the new requirements?

For PSHE and citizenship at key stages 1 and 2 the new requirements are in the form of a non-statutory framework and are found in *The National Curriculum, Handbook for Primary Teachers in England. Key Stages 1 and 2* (QCA/DfEE, 1999). The framework is designed to build on and extend current good practice and provide opportunities for all pupils to learn and achieve. The learning framework will enable schools to prepare their pupils for the opportunities, responsibilities and experiences of life through more explicit and coherent provision in the area of citizenship. It will also help to ensure continuity and progression of learning. (Note that the QCA's new scheme of work (QCA, 2000) provides guidance to help schools implement the proposals.)

The learning framework aims to enable schools to:

- promote pupils' personal and social development, including their health and well-being, effectively;

- develop pupils' knowledge and understanding of their role and responsibilities as active citizens in a modern democracy;

- equip them with the values, skills and knowledge to deal with difficult moral and social questions they face.

The framework allows schools to develop their own approach to the teaching of citizenship and recognises the integrated approach which most primary schools already have to teaching and learning in these areas.

The non-statutory guidelines at key stages 1 and 2 (QCA/DfEE, 1999) are divided into two main sections – knowledge, skills and understanding; and breadth of opportunity. The former is divided into four sub-sections:

- developing confidence and responsibility and making the most of their abilities;
- preparing to play an active role as citizens;
- developing a healthy, safer lifestyle;
- developing good relationships and respecting the differences between people.

Some links to other curriculum subjects, both core and non-core subjects, have been teased out and are located in the margins of the Order (QCA/DfEE, 1999).

Ways in which primary geography may support citizenship education

'...learning about other people and becoming aware of problems don't in themselves change anything. Young people may go through a range of emotional as well as intellectual responses; they may feel sad, angry, enraged, outraged or frustrated. Yet unless they are given the opportunity to develop relevant skills as well as planning avenues for taking action, they will feel increasingly powerless.' (Oxfam, 1999)

Some important planning principles should be followed in order to avoid the problems described in the above quotation:

- To ensure that the children feel total involvement with and ownership of the issue under review, the ideas and foci must come from a genuine concern felt and expressed by *them*, not their teacher.
- The children must be encouraged to gain information and knowledge on the issue so that they can make informed decisions which are based on reliable data and facts, and which take account of the views of all who are affected by the issue.
- The children must be listened to and their views taken seriously. Consultation must be real, participation active; children should not be consulted and then ignored.
- Children should be encouraged to express their own point of view, to challenge the views of others, to negotiate and to compromise, and to make individual and group decisions as appropriate.
- Children need to be taught the value of weighing up all the evidence and the consequences before making any decision, and that responsibility follows actions.
- Children need to be aware that in certain circumstances some actions are more appropriate and likely to succeed than others, and that there are limitations to what individuals can do.
- Children should be aware that change can happen at different levels: individual, local, national, global.

Assessment presents particular issues for citizenship because of the significance of the pupils' own attitudes and values. However, it is important that teachers do assess pupils' learning so that appropriate activities can be planned. Education for citizenship does have a knowledge base and this can be assessed, together with understanding. Pupils' ability to use their knowledge and understanding can also be assessed (see the QCA (2000) scheme of work document for guidance on this issue).

Figure 1 describes in detail links between the PSHE/citizenship framework, sustainable development, the geography programme of study and the QCA scheme of work for geography. This grid will help you to audit your current provision and to identify additional opportunities. However, it is not intended that you deliver all opportunities, rather that you select a manageable number to enhance both the teaching and learning of geography and the PSHE/citizenship framework.

Figure 2 shows how citizenship activities can be added to an existing scheme of work. Again, it would only be necessary to develop a manageable number of these over the course of the unit.

Figure 1: Links between PSHE/citizenship, sustainable development and geography.

Links between PSHE/citizenship, sustainable development and geography – key stage 1 (non-statutory guidance)

During key stage 1, pupils learn about themselves as developing individuals and members of communities, building on their own experiences and on the early learning goals for personal, social and emotional development. They learn the basic rules and skills for keeping themselves healthy and safe and for behaving well. They have opportunities to show they can take some responsibility for themselves and their environment. They begin to learn about their own and others' feelings and become aware of the views, needs and rights of other of children and older people. As members of a class and school community, they learn social skills such as how to share, take turns, help others, resolve simple arguments and resist bullying. They begin to take an active part in the life of their school and its neighbourhood.

KNOWLEDGE, SKILLS & UNDERSTANDING	Links to KS1 geography	Dimensions	QCA's scheme of work. Links and units	Geography activities linked to citizenship,
Developing confidence and responsibility and making the most of their abilities	POS		for potential extension and development to support citizenship education	PSHE and sustainable development
1. Pupils should be taught:				
1a. to recognise what they like and dislike, what is fair and unfair, and what is right and wrong	Gg/3a, b, d	PEOPLE and VIEWPOINTS	UNITS 1, 2, 3, 4, 5	E.g. impact of change on people's lives (e.g. use Katie Morag and the New Pier, industrial pollution)
1b. to share their opinions on things that matter to them and explain their views	Gg/1c	FUTURES PEOPLE and VIEWPOINTS	UNITS 1, 2, 3, 4, 5	LOCAL ISSUES, including sustainable development e.g. pollution, traffic, redevelopment of derelict land, develop-ment of school grounds
1c. to recognise, name and deal with their feelings in a positive way	Gg/ 1d	PEOPLE AND VIEWPOINTS	UNIT 1	LOCAL ISSUES e.g. pollution, traffic and safe routes to school, redevelopment of derelict land, develop-ment of school grounds
1d. to think about themselves, learn from their experiences and recognise what they are good at				LOCAL ISSUES, including sustainable development
1e. how to set simple goals.				

KNOWLEDGE, SKILLS & UNDERSTANDING *Preparing to play an active role as citizens*	Links to KS1 geography POS	Dimensions	QCA's scheme of work. Links and units for potential extension and development to support citizenship education	Geography activities linked to citizenship, PSHE and sustainable development
2. Pupils should be taught:				
2a. to take part in discussions with one other person and the whole class	Gg/ 1a, c, d, 2a, 3a, b, c, d	FUTURES PEOPLE AND VIEWPOINTS	UNITS 1, 2, 3, 4, 5	LOCAL AND GLOBAL ISSUES, including sustainable development – circle time, role play
2b. to take part in simple debate about topical issues	Gg/1c, 2b, 4a, 5b	CHANGE FUTURES PEOPLE AND VIEWPOINTS	UNITS 1, 2, 3, 5	LOCAL AND GLOBAL ISSUES, including sustainable development – ROLE PLAY: waste/pollution/ safe routes to school
2c. to recognise choices they can make, and recognise the difference between right and wrong	Gg/ 1c, 4a, 5a, b	CHANGE PEOPLE AND VIEWPOINTS	UNITS 1, 2, 3, 4	LOCAL AND GLOBAL ISSUES, including sustainable development – dropping litter, wasteful use of scarce resources
2d. to agree and follow rules for their group and classroom, and understand how rules help them	Gg/2b	CHOICES AND DECISIONS	UNITS 1, 2, 3	LOCAL AND GLOBAL ISSUES, including sustainable development – dropping litter, wasteful use of scarce resources
2e. to realise that people and other living things have needs, and that they have responsibilities to meet them	Gg/1a, c, 3c, 4a, 5a, b	CONTEXT CHANGE FUTURES	UNITS 1, 2, 3	LOCAL AND GLOBAL ISSUES, including sustainable development – wants and needs, safety in environment, etc.
2f. that they belong to various groups and communities, such as family and school	Gg/3c, d, e, 5a, b 6a, b, 7a, b	CONTEXT PEOPLE AND VIEWPOINTS	UNITS 1, 2, 3	LOCAL ISSUES
2g. what improves and harms their local, natural and built environments and about some of the ways people look after them	Gg/1c, 5	CONTEXT CHANGE FUTURES PEOPLE AND VIEWPOINTS	UNITS 1, 2, 3, 4	LOCAL AND GLOBAL ISSUES – pollution, dropping litter, wasteful use of scarce resources, safety in environment, etc.

KNOWLEDGE, SKILLS & UNDERSTANDING	Links to KS1 geography POS	Dimensions	QCA's scheme of work. Links and units for potential extension and development to support citizenship education	Geography activities linked to citizenship, PSHE and sustainable development
2h. to contribute to the life of the class and school	Gg/ 2b, 7b	PEOPLE AND VIEWPOINTS UNITS 1, 2		
2i. to realise that money comes from different sources and can be used for different purposes.		CHANGE		DAY VISITS, LOCAL AREA DEVELOPMENT
Developing a healthy, safer lifestyle 3. Pupils should be taught				
3a. how to make simple choices to improve their health and well-being		CHOICES AND DECISIONS, PEOPLE AND VIEWPOINTS	UNITS 1, 2	FIELDWORK, LOCAL ISSUES
3b. to maintain personal hygiene		CHOICES AND DECISIONS		FIELDWORK VISITS, LOCAL ISSUES
3c. how some diseases can be spread and can be controlled		CHANGE, CHOICES AND DECISIONS		
3d. about the process of growing from young to old and how people's needs change		CHANGE		LOCAL ISSUES, ENVIRONMENTAL CHANGE
3e. the names of the main body parts		CHANGE		
3g. rules for, and ways of, keeping safe, including basic road safety, and about people who can help them to stay safe	Gg/ 2b, 5a, b, 7a, b	PEOPLE AND VIEWPOINTS	UNITS 1, 2	FIELDWORK – SAFETY
Developing good relationships and respecting the differences between people 4. Pupils should be taught:				
4a. to recognise how their behaviour affects other people	Gg/ 1c, 5a, b	PEOPLE AND VIEWPOINTS	UNITS 1, 2, 4, 5	LOCAL ISSUES, COMMUNITY ISSUES, FAIR TRADE
4b. to listen to other people, and play and work co-operatively	Gg/ 1c, 2b, 7b	PEOPLE AND VIEWPOINTS FUTURES	UNITS 1, 2	LOCAL ISSUES, COMMUNITY ISSUES
4c. to identify and respect the differences and similarities between people	Gg/ 3a, b, c, d, e, 6a, b	PEOPLE AND VIEWPOINTS FUTURES	UNITS 3, 5	LOCAL ISSUES

BREADTH OF OPPORTUNITY	Links to KS1 geography POS	Dimensions	QCA's scheme of work. Links and units for potential extension and development to support citizenship education	Geography activities linked to citizenship, PSHE and sustainable development
5. During the key stage, pupils should be taught the **knowledge, skills and understanding** through opportunities to:				
5a. take and share responsibility (e.g. for their own behaviour; by helping make classroom rules and following them; by looking after pets well)	Gg/ 2b, 5a, b	PEOPLE AND VIEWPOINTS	UNITS 1, 2	LOCAL ISSUES
5b. feel positive about themselves (for example, by having their achievements recognised and by being given positive feedback about themselves)		PEOPLE AND VIEWPOINTS		LOCAL ISSUES
5c. take part in discussions (for example, talking about topics of school, local, national, European, Commonwealth and global concern, such as 'Where do food and raw materials for industry come from?')	Gg/ 1a, c, d, 2a, e, 5a, b, 7a	PEOPLE AND VIEWPOINTS	UNITS 1, 2, 4, 5	ROLE PLAY, ENVIRONMENTAL ISSUES, FAIR TRADE, CONNECTIONS, SUSTAINABLE DEVELOPMENT
5d. make real choices (for example, between healthy options in school meals, what to watch on television, what game to play, how to spend and save money sensibly)		PEOPLE AND VIEWPOINTS	UNITS 2, 5	
5e. meet and talk with people (for example, with outside visitors such as religious leaders, police officers, the school nurse)	Gg/ 1a, 2b, 4a, 5a, b, 7b	PEOPLE AND VIEWPOINTS	UNITS 2, 5	FIELDWORK, WORK-ING WITH PEOPLE FROM DIFFERENT WALKS OF LIFE
5f. develop relationships through work and play (for example, by sharing equipment with other pupils or their friends in a group task)	Gg/ 1a, b, 2b, 7b		UNITS 1, 2, 5	
5g. consider social or moral dilemmas that they come across in everyday life (for example, aggressive behaviour, questions of fairness, right and wrong, simple political issues, use of money, simple environmental issues)	Gg/ 3c, 5a, b	PEOPLE AND VIEWPOINTS	UNITS 1, 2, 4, 5	LOCAL ISSUES, DEVELOPMENTS OF SCHOOL GROUNDS, POVERTY, WATER ISSUES, EDUCATION, FAIR TRADE, SUSTAINABLE DEVELOPMENT
5h. ask for help (for example, from family and friends, mid-day supervisors, older pupils, the police)	2b, 5a	PEOPLE AND VIEWPOINTS		WORKING WITH PEOPLE FROM DIFFERENT WALKS OF LIFE

Links between PSHE/citizenship, sustainable development and geography – key stage 2 (non-statutory guidance)

During key stage 2, pupils learn about themselves as growing and changing individuals with their own experiences and ideas, and as members of their communities. They become more mature, independent and self confident. They learn about the wider world and the interdependence of communities within it. They develop their sense of social and moral responsibility and begin to understand that their own choices and behaviour can affect local, national or global issues and political and social institutions. They learn how to take part more fully in school and community activities. As they begin to develop into young adults, they face the changes of puberty and transfer to secondary school with support and encouragement from their school. They learn how to make confident and informed choices about their health and environment; to take more responsibility, individually and as a group, for their own learning; and to resist bullying.

KNOWLEDGE, SKILLS & UNDERSTANDING *Developing confidence and responsibility and making the most of their abilities* 1. Pupils should be taught:	Links to KS2 geography POS	Dimensions	QCA's scheme of work. Links and units for potential extension and development to support citizenship education	Geography activities linked to citizenship, PSHE and sustainable development
1a. to talk and write about their opinions, and explain their views on issues that affect themselves and society	Gg/ 1a, b, c, d, e, 2a, d, f, g 3c, f, 5a, b, 6c, d, e	PEOPLE AND VIEWPOINTS	UNITS 6, 19, 20	LOCAL ISSUES pertinent to children, school and community ISSUES in EDCs GLOBAL ISSUES, including sustainable development – global warming, pollution etc.
1b. to recognise their worth as individuals by identifying positive things about themselves and their achievements, seeing their mistakes, making amends and setting personal goals			UNITS 6, 19, 20	
1c. to face new challenges positively by collecting information, looking for help, making responsible choices and taking action	Gg/ 5a, b, 6d, e	CHOICES AND DECISIONS	ALL UNITS (e.g. 9, 20, new unit on coasts)	LOCAL ISSUES, including sustainable development – SITING of new developments – housing, industry, use of green/brownfield sites, urban regeneration
1d. to recognise, as they approach puberty, how people's emotions change at that time and how to deal with their feelings towards themselves, their family and others in a positive way				
1e. about the range of jobs carried out by people they know and to understand how they can develop skills to make their own contribution in the future	Gg/1d, e, 2g, 3g, 5a, b, d, e	FUTURES	UNITS 8, 13 New unit on coasts	LOCAL ISSUES pertinent to children, school and community ISSUES in EDCs GLOBAL ISSUES, including sustainable lifestyles: waste disposal, global warming etc. INDUSTRY LINKS TOURISM

KNOWLEDGE, SKILLS & UNDERSTANDING	Links to KS2 geography POS	Dimensions	QCA's scheme of work. Links and units for potential extension and development to support citizenship education	Geography activities linked to citizenship, PSHE and sustainable development
1f. to look after their money and realise that future wants and needs may be met through saving	Gg/ 3g, 6a, b	FUTURES	UNIT 18	
Preparing to play an active role as citizens 2. Pupils should be taught:				
2a. to research, to discuss and debate topical issues, problems and events	Gg/ 1a, b, c, d, e, 2a, b, c, d, e, f, g, 3e, f, g, 4b, 5a, b, 6a, b, d, e, 7a, b	CONTEXT	UNIT 6	LOCAL ISSUES pertinent to children and school ISSUES in EDCs GLOBAL ISSUES TOURISM (respect for culture and lifestyle of others), SUSTAINABLE DEVELOPMENT - discuss and debate commitment to a sustainable world (quality of life/standard of living)
2b. why and how rules and laws are made and enforced, why different rules are needed in different situations and how to take part in making and changing rules		CHOICES AND DECISIONS	UNIT 8	LOCAL ISSUES pertinent to children and school – local, regional, national government) – LITTER/WASTE/ POLLUTION TOURISM (respect for culture and lifestyle of others and linked to sustainable lifestyles)
2c. to realise the consequences of anti-social and aggressive behaviours, such as bullying and racism, on individuals and communities		PEOPLE AND VIEWPOINTS	UNIT 8	LOCAL ISSUES pertinent to needs of elderly, very young, etc. ISSUES in EDCs GLOBAL ISSUES TOURISM (respect for culture and lifestyle of others)
2d. that there are different kinds of responsibilities, rights and duties at home, at school and in the community, and that these sometime conflict with each other	Gg/ 1d, 2g, 3e, g, 5a, b, 6d, e, 7a, b	PEOPLE AND VIEWPOINTS	UNITS 8, 11, 12, 13, 17, 20, 21	LOCAL ISSUES pertinent to children and school SUSTAINABLE DEVELOPMENT – AGENDA 21 and ECO-SCHOOLS

KNOWLEDGE, SKILLS & UNDERSTANDING	Links to KS2 geography POS	Dimensions	QCA's scheme of work. Links and units for potential extension and development to support citizenship education	Geography activities linked to citizenship, PSHE and sustainable development
2e. to reflect on spiritual, moral, social and cultural issues, using imagination to understand other people's experiences	Gg/ 5a, b, 6e	PEOPLE AND VIEWPOINTS	UNIT 10, 14	EDC
2f. to resolve differences by looking at alternatives, making decisions and explaining choices	Gg/ 1d, e, 2g	CHOICES AND DECISIONS	UNITS 8, 11, 12, 13, 17, 20, 21	ENVIRONMENTAL ISSUES AND SUSTAINABLE DEVELOPMENT– assessing quality of the environment
2g. what democracy is, and about the basic institutions that support it locally and nationally	Gg/ 1d, e, 2g, 6e, 7a, b	PEOPLE AND VIEWPOINTS CHOICES AND DECISIONS	UNITS 8, 11, 12, 13, 17, 20, 21	LOCAL ISSUES pertinent to children and school ISSUES in EDCs GLOBAL ISSUES TOURISM (respect for culture and lifestyle of others)
2h. to recognise the role of voluntary, community and pressure groups	Gg/ 1d	CHOICES AND DECISIONS	UNITS 8, 11, 12, 13, 17, 20, 21	LOCAL ISSUES pertinent to children and school (recycling, waste minimisation) ISSUES in EDCs (work of aid agencies) GLOBAL ISSUES including sustainable development – AGENDA 21, ECO-SCHOOLS TOURISM (respect for culture and lifestyle of others)
2i. to appreciate the range of national, regional, religious and ethnic identities in the UK	Gg/ 3f, 6a, d, 7a, b	CHOICES AND DECISIONS		LOCAL ISSUES pertinent to children and school TOURISM (respect for culture and lifestyle of others)
2j. that resources can be allocated in different ways and that these economic choices affect individuals, communities and the sustainability of the environment	Gg/ 5a, b		UNITS 6, 8, 11, 12, 13, 17, 20, 21	SUSTAINABLE DEVELOPMENT – waste disposal, use of finite resources, food production AGENDA 21, ECO-SCHOOLS

KNOWLEDGE, SKILLS & UNDERSTANDING	Links to KS2 geography POS	Dimensions	QCA's scheme of work. Links and units for potential extension and development to support citizenship education	Geography activities linked to citizenship, PSHE and sustainable development
2k. to explore how the media present information.		PEOPLE AND VIEWPOINTS	UNITS 14, 16, 18	LOCAL ISSUES pertinent to children and school GLOBAL ISSUES (floods, droughts) TOURISM (respect for culture and lifestyle of others)
Developing a healthy, safer lifestyle 3. Pupils should be taught:				
3a. what makes a healthy lifestyle, including the benefits of exercise and healthy eating, what affects mental health, and how to make informed choices.	Gg/ 2b, g, 3e, 6a, 7a, b, c	CHOICES AND DECISIONS	UNITS 13, 14	FIELDWORK VISITS health, exercise and physical conditions for fieldwork visit
3b. that bacteria and viruses can affect health and that following simple, safe routines can reduce their spread	Gg/ 5a, b, 6a, c, e, 7a, b, c	CONTEXT	UNITS 14, 20	FIELDWORK VISITS – river, farm, residential visits, health and safety, protective clothing etc.
3c. about how the body changes as they approach puberty		CONTEXT		RESIDENTIAL FIELDWORK VISITS
3d. which commonly available substances and drugs are legal and illegal, their effects and their risks		CHOICES AND DECISIONS		SAFETY AT HOME, IN LOCAL ENVIRONMENT
3e. to recognise the different risks in different situations and then decide how to behave responsibly, including sensible road use, and judging what kind of physical contact is acceptable or unacceptable	Gg/ 2b, 7c	CHOICES AND DECISIONS	UNITS 14, 15	FIELDWORK and off-school site visits. Safety in the workplace, in local environment, etc.
3f. that pressure to behave in an unacceptable or risky way can come from a variety of sources, including people they know, and how to ask for help and use basic techniques for resisting pressure to do wrong	Gg/ 2b, 7c	CHOICES AND DECISIONS		FIELDWORK VISITS AND LOCAL STUDIES
3g. school rules about health and safety, basic emergency aid procedures and where to get help	Gg/ 2b, 7c	CHOICES AND DECISIONS, PEOPLE AND VIEWPOINTS	UNITS 12, 14, 15, 20, 21	FIELDWORK AND RESIDENTIAL VISITS

KNOWLEDGE, SKILLS & UNDERSTANDING *Developing good relationships and respecting the differences between people* 4. Pupils should be taught:	Links to KS2 geography POS	Dimensions	QCA's scheme of work. Links and units for potential extension and development to support citizenship education	Geography activities linked to citizenship, PSHE and sustainable development
4a. that their actions affect themselves and others, to care about other people's feelings and to try to see things from their points of view	Gg/ 1d, e, 3e, f, g, 5a, b	PEOPLE AND VIEWPOINTS CONTEXT	UNITS 15, 18	ISSUES IN LOCAL AREA, IN CONTRASTING LOCALITIES (EDCs)
4b. to think about the lives of other people living in other places and times, and people with different values and customs	Gg/3a, d, e, f, g, 6a, b, 7a, b	PEOPLE AND VIEWPOINTS	UNITS 10, 18	ISSUES IN LOCAL AREA, IN CONTRASTING LOCALITIES (EDCs)
4c. to be aware of different types of relationship, including marriage and those between friends and families, and to develop skills to be effective in relationships				
4d. to realise the nature and consequences of racism, teasing, bullying, and aggressive behaviours, and how to respond to them and ask for help	Gg/ 1d, 3d, e, f, g, 6a, b		UNIT 10	EDCs
4e. to recognise and challenge stereotypes	Gg/ 3f, g, 6a, b, 7a, b	PEOPLE AND VIEWPOINTS CHOICES AND DECISIONS	UNITS 10, 18	EDCs
4f. that differences and similarities between people arise from a number of factors, including cultural, ethnic, racial, religious diversity, gender and disability	Gg/ 3g, 6a, b, 7a, b	PEOPLE AND VIEWPOINTS CHOICES AND DECISIONS	UNITS 10, 18	CONTRASTING LOCALITIES AND EDCs
4g. where individuals, families and groups can get help and support for				
BREADTH OF OPPORTUNITY				
5. During the key stage, pupils should be taught the **knowledge, skills and understanding** through opportunities to:				
5a. take responsibility (for example, for planning and looking after the school environment; for the needs of others, such as by acting as peer supporter, as a befriender, or as a playground mediator for younger pupils; for looking after animals properly; for identifying safe, healthy and sustainable means of travel when planning their journey to school)	Gg/ 1e, 2g, 3e, g, 5a, b, 6d, e, 7a, b	PEOPLE AND VIEWPOINTS	UNITS 6, 8, 11, 12, 13, 17, 20, 21	DEVELOPING THE SCHOOL GROUNDS – map work (using and making), field sketches, weather, site, situation, aspect, questionnaire about type of development, involvement AGENDA 21, ECO-SCHOOLS

BREADTH OF OPPORTUNITY	Links to KS2 geography POS	Dimensions	QCA's scheme of work. Links and units for potential extension and development to support citizenship education	Geography activities linked to citizenship, PSHE and sustainable development
5b. feel positive about themselves (for example, by producing personal diaries, profiles and portfolios of achievements; by having opportunities to show what they can do and how much responsibility they can take)	Gg/ 1e, 2g, 3e, g, 5a, b, 6d, e, 7a, b			RESIDENTIAL VISITS
5c. participate (for example, in the school's decision-making process, relating it to democratic structures and processes such as councils, parliaments, government and voting)	Gg/ 1d, e, 2g, 3e, g, 5a, b, 6e	CHOICES AND DECISIONS	UNITS 6, 8, 11, 12, 13, 17, 20, 21	LOCAL ISSUES pertinent to children and school – traffic, park, pollution etc. 'Put it to your MP/local councillor/ local planner' type activities.
5d. make real choices and decisions (for example, about issues affecting their health and well-being such as smoking; on the use of scarce resources; how to spend money, including pocket money and contributions to charities)	Gg/ 1d, e, 2g, 3e, g, 5a, b, 6e	CHANGE CHOICES AND DECISIONS	UNITS 8, 1, 12, 13, 20	GREEN ISSUES, including sustainable development – use of scarce resources, burning fossil fuels, greenhouse effect, acid rain LOCAL ISSUES – as above, waste disposal, dog mess in park, exhaust fumes, etc.
5e. meet and talk with people (for example, people who contribute to society through environmental pressure groups or international aid organisations; people who work in school and the neighbourhood, such as religious leaders, community police officers)	Gg/ 1d, 2g, 3e, g, 5a, b, 6e	PEOPLE AND VIEWPOINTS CHOICES AND DECISIONS	UNITS 6, 8, 13, 20	LOCAL ISSUES – involvement of planners, councillors, environmental groups to listen to their views and question them
5f. develop relationships through work and play (for example, taking part in activities with groups that have particular needs, such as children with special needs and the elderly; communicating with children in other countries by satellite, e-mail or letters)	Gg/ 1e, 2a, b, d, f, g, 5a, b, 6e	CHANGE	UNITS 12, 16, 18, 20	LOCAL ISSUES pertinent to children and school and local community – safe routes to school, cycleways, services for the elderly, etc. Communicating information about own locality to another locality and vice versa

BREADTH OF OPPORTUNITY	Links to KS2 geography POS	Dimensions	QCA's scheme of work. Links and units for potential extension and development to support citizenship education	Geography activities linked to citizenship, PSHE and sustainable development
5g. consider social and moral dilemmas that they come across in life (for example, including respect and understanding between different races and dealing with harassment)	Gg/ 6a, b, 7a, b	CONTEXT	UNITS 10, 12, 20	TOURISM (respect for culture and lifestyle of others)
5h. find information and advice (for example, through help lines; by understanding about welfare systems in society)	Gg/ 1d, e, 6e	CHANGE		TOURISM WASTE – disposal/ recycling, etc.
5i. prepare for change (for example, transferring to secondary school)		CHANGE		

Figure 2: Example of a key stage 1 planning matrix, based on Unit 5 'Where in the world is Barnaby Bear?' in QCA/DfEE (1998) – with citizenship activities added.

ENQUIRY QUESTIONS	LEARNING OBJECTIVES	POSSIBLE TEACHING ACTIVITIES	LEARNING OUTCOMES	POINTS TO NOTE
Where has Barnaby Bear travelled to this week or month?	▪ to locate a variety of places at home and abroad	▪ Arrange for Barnaby Bear to be taken with parents, children, staff or governors when they visit places away from school, and for him to send postcards back to school or be photographed in these places.	▪ identify a variety of places around the world ▪ begin to understand the concept of visiting other places ▪ understand that other places may be different from their own locality	**PSHE/citizenship activities** – Role play. Use role-play areas (e.g. travel agency, airport check-in desk) to introduce the world of work.
Can we find these places on a map?	▪ to find places on a map	▪ With the children's help, create a wall display of the postcards and photographs and a series of maps that identify Barnaby's destinations. Lower attaining children may be asked to sort the cards or photographs into labelled piles, e.g. local/not local, like/don't like, sunny/cloudy. ▪ Arrange for each class to take on the role of looking after Barnaby's corner or 'home' for a time. He needs a suitable home to be constructed in a prominent place.		**PSHE/citizenship activities** – Promote world/racial harmony through locating and discussing places where Barnaby has visited. Design and technology: if the children are involved in designing and building a home for Barnaby, there are links with design and technology.

ENQUIRY QUESTIONS	LEARNING OBJECTIVES	POSSIBLE TEACHING ACTIVITIES	LEARNING OUTCOMES	POINTS TO NOTE
What will it be like when Barnaby is there?	▪ to recognise features of places ▪ identify types of weather experienced in places and seasonal change and how they affect people	▪ Ask the children to describe what the places Barnaby visits are like and what sort of weather he might have experienced, using the postcards and photographs received. ▪ With the children's help, set up a holiday table near the display. Ask children to choose, for example, the type of weather gear he may need for each place he visits and decide whether he needs his passport. ▪ Ask the traveller who took Barnaby either to write a short diary or provide a weather report. Ask the children to compare this with what they thought the weather would be like. ▪ Create a display of simple artefacts to show the life of the country visited, e.g. a newspaper, coins, food packaging and other everyday things.	▪ show an interest in the world around them ▪ develop a deeper understanding of the notion of travel to other places ▪ understand that weather conditions in other countries may be different from those they are experiencing at the same time ▪ are aware of similarities and differences between other countries and their own	**PSHE/citizenship activities** – Ask the children to help Barnaby pack his suitcase. **PSHE/citizenship activities** – Ask the children how Barnaby can keep himself safe while on holiday. Write a safety code for Barnaby. History: using artefacts from different countries.
How did Barnaby travel to these places?	▪ about the location of other places ▪ about the types of transport used to get to other places	▪ Ask the children to look at pictures of Barnaby using different types of transport and the places he visited and, for each, say whether it is a long way away, whether he would have to cross sea, mountains or rivers, or drive along a motorway, and then decide what would be the best way for him to travel to the place. ▪ Ask the children to draw a graph to show the number of times Barnaby used different types of transport in a given time and find out which type of transport he used most. ▪ Ask the children to think about how long the journeys took him.	▪ develop a sense of distance associated with travel ▪ know about different ways of travelling to places ▪ know that different types of transport will give different travel times	Mathematics: these activities could link with work on classifying, representing and interpreting data, and understanding and using measures. **PSHE/citizenship activities** – Discuss the behaviour of a 'good' holiday maker and a 'bad' holidaymaker. Give each group of children a collection of photographs (images of tourists behaving as 'good tourists', showing respect, and images of tourist showing no respect for the host population or their culture). Ask the children to put the photographs into two piles – good tourist behaviour/bad tourist behaviour. Ask the children to draw a cartoon strip which shows Barnaby behaving like a good holidaymaker and Barnaby behaving like a bad holidaymaker. Write a code of behaviour for Barnaby.

Teaching methods and learning activities

It is widely accepted that children learn in different ways, so a wide range of methodologies should be employed. Engaging children's interest through active learning is a very effective way of making the learning experience more memorable and effective. The activities planned must be designed to help the children develop the knowledge, skills and understanding to enable them to act as responsible citizens, whether the issue has a local or global dimension. Teaching and learning strategies must encompass a wide variety of activities, from children working as individuals, to pair, group and whole-class activities, as shown below.

For all issues, whether local, national or global, children need to develop strategies to find out who has the power to make changes and identify the stakeholders who can influence the decision makers. Pupils also need to consider who should be informed about the issue - there will be different people for different issues (Figure 3).

Figure 3: Issues and action.

Examples of issues	Who has the power?	Who can influence the decision (stakeholders)?	Action the children can take (depending on the issue)
Development of the school grounds	■ Governors of the school ■ Head Teacher	■ Children, staff (both teaching and non-teaching), parents, local community	■ Research – seek out evidence ■ Undertake an audit (e.g. green audit of school) ■ Collect information ■ Analyse and present data from evidence collected
Siting of factory, supermarket etc.	■ Board of Directors of a Company or the Managing Director ■ Local councillors ■ Parish councillors ■ Planning Dept. of local authority	■ Local people – individually, collectively ■ Voters, Local constituents ■ Customers ■ Staff of a company ■ Shareholders of a company ■ Local action groups ■ Local media	■ Find out the opinions of others – questionnaires, debates (e.g. other shopkeepers' and customers' opinions of siting of new supermarket) ■ Talk, discuss and inform (e.g. discuss with the Governors of the school proposed development of school grounds; discuss fair trade issues and rights of children in EDCs with the Board of Directors of a local supermarket)
Siting of new houses, new roads etc. – any thing that has an impact on the local community	■ Local councillors ■ Parish councillors ■ Planning Dept. of local authority ■ Highways Dept.	■ Local people – individually, collectively ■ Voters, local constituents ■ Local action groups ■ Local media	■ Inform interested parties (those who will be affected) ■ Put forward the case in a rational, informed manner (e.g. reasons for and/or against the site of a proposed new factory to members of local planning department) ■ Write letters in the persuasive and/or discussion genre to people who have the power to make changes (e.g. persuasive letters to local council about upgrading the local playground)
Issues that impact on the whole country	■ Nationally – Government – politicians	■ Voters, Action groups (e.g. Friends of the Earth, Save our ...... action groups) ■ media – local/national	■ Draw up petitions ■ Make posters ■ Display their work in libraries/town halls/ information entries etc.
Issues that have an impact on Europe	■ Europe – European Parliament and European politicians	■ Voters ■ Action groups ■ Media – local/national/ European	■ Inform people who need to know the opinions of those people who will be/are affected (e.g. local councillors about the opinions of local people about the closure of the local leisure centre or change of use of a park)
Issues that have an impact on the world	■ Global/world leaders and politicians	■ Voters ■ Action groups ■ Media – local/national/world	■ Contact the media – local press ■ Invite an MP/local councillor into school ■ Hold sponsored events ■ Create and sell a fair trade directory for their area (e.g. to make others aware of goods which are produced fairly in EDCs, where the workers have good working conditions and fair pay for their work)

Teaching activities

All teaching activities can be adapted to study other issues – not just the ones identified in this chapter.

An example of a key stage 2 activity

Issue: A hotel development on a tropical beach and/or in a rainforest

This activity helps children to explore the impact of tourism on a community. Communities are diverse and the various sectors within them are affected by tourist development in different ways. Through the activity, the children are helped to recognise that change can have both positive and negative effects on different sectors of a community. The activity places the children in a variety of roles. Concepts of fair play, power relationships and invasion of territory are explored with the aim of extending their knowledge and understanding of people and places.

This activity is linked to a book called *Where the Forest Meets the Sea* by Jeanie Baker (Baker, 1989), but can easily be used in other contexts. This is a story about a day trip when a boy and his father take a boat to reach a tropical beach and an ancient rainforest, Daintree Rainforest in North Queensland, Australia. This fascinating and innovative picture book chronicles the reflections of the young boy as he imagines what the rainforest was like in the past and how it might change in the future. The relief collage illustrations, constructed from a multitude of natural materials, create a stunning 3D effect, bringing together visions of the past, present and future.

The book raises a host of issues to do with environmental change; past/present/ future; land use. (Note: The teaching activities that follow here can easily be adapted for other development situations, e.g. new supermarket, bypass, building or extending a regional airport, siting of a landfill site.

- Locate the rainforest on a globe. Locate other rainforests. Name the continents in which the rainforests are located.
- Discuss the features of the rainforest, including vegetation, animals and their habitats, land use, etc.
- Discuss the issues facing tropical beaches/rainforests. **(citizenship activity)**
- Create a rainforest environment with trees, birds and animals made from bright materials (in role-play area).
- What are the ethics of the boy and his father visiting the rainforest but implicitly criticising more organised tourism. **(citizenship activity)**
- Arrange children in groups of three or four and give each one a photograph of an unspoilt tropical beach scene. Ask them the following questions: What is this place like? How could this place be changing? Why is it like it is? How do you feel about this place? Who might use the area shown in the photograph? These questions involve the children in considering, describing and explaining the concepts of continuity and change, and expressing their views in relation to the place on the photograph. Share responses with the whole class. **(citizenship activity)**
- Who decides if there is to be a hotel on the beach? Who will benefit and who might lose from tourism? **(citizenship activity)**
- Discuss arguments for and against the development of tourism in this area of tropical beach/rainforest. Who is for the development and why – which people/groups of people? Who is against the development and why – which people/groups of people? **(citizenship activity)**

- What things will change on the beach/in the rainforest? Why? How do you feel about the changes? How do you think the native Australians (Aborigines) feel about the changes? (Encourage the children to express views about these changes) **(citizenship activity)**

- What impact will the development of tourism have on the environment? **(citizenship activity)**

- Ask children to study the photograph of the unspoilt tropical beach and to discuss who might use it. In roles, debate the issue of building a new holiday complex on the tropical beach and the changes it will bring. Which people are for the changes and which are against? Characters could be: Melanie Forest (Conservationist), Darren Plant (Botanist), Lesley Fortune (Director of Grandiose Hotel Developments Ltd.), Peter Campaign (Town Councillor), Jeremy Beach (Barrier Reef Coastal Ranger), Miranda Holidayinn (Midsummer Hotel), Danny (the local boy), Polly (Windsurfing Club), Melanie Law (Local Resident) etc. **(citizenship activity)**

- The children can undertake the same activity as in the unit on coasts in the QCA scheme of work (QCA/DfEE, 2000) but with the roles changed to be applicable to this environment and this development (Figure 4). The activity is the same. **(citizenship activity)**

- Use a writing frame to put forward the cases for and against the building of the new holiday complex (note taking, discussion and/or persuasion genre) **(citizenship and literacy activities) (Figure 5).**

- Make a tourist map and brochures advertising a visit to the rainforest hotel. Include all the information and pictures of what you can see and do. **(citizenship and literacy activities)**

Development activities for key stage 2

The aim of this activity is to investigate the value of developments to the people affected by identifying and asking environmental, economic, social and political questions.

- Introduce the children to the Development Compass Rose (Development Education Centre, Birmingham) – Natural, Economic, Social and Who decides (political)? (Figure 6). This framework helps children to discuss a range of issues (issues either identified by the teacher as part of the area of study or by children themselves). It can be applied to any issue, resource, photograph or artefact either at a local, regional, national or international scale. **(citizenship activity)**

- Use the four points of the Development Compass Rose to focus the children's questioning of a photograph of an issue. (Stick photograph in centre of page and ask children to write questions about it around the photograph.) Help the children refine and sharpen their questioning. Use the children's questions to start the enquiry process. **(citizenship activity)**

- Geographical issues which could be discussed, using the Development Compass Rose as a focus, are: closure of local shop/local school, suspension of local bus service, building of a new shopping mall, impact of developers from developed countries on indigenous population of an EDC. **(citizenship activity)**

  Example A: building of a new shopping mall (e.g. Cheshire Oaks near Chester, and its impact on the shopkeepers in Chester and Ellesmere Port). Who decided to build this shopping complex here? Is it more expensive to buy things here or in the town/city centres? Who owns the complex? **(citizenship activity)**

  Example B: development of a tourist centre on a remote tropical beach (see previous activity). **(citizenship activity)**

ROLE PLAY (citizenship activity)

- Ask children to study a photograph of an unspoilt tropical beach/coastal environment and to discuss who might use it.

- Divide children into six groups, each to assume one of the following roles: local resident/local fisherfolk/local child/local government official/travel company representative/holidaymaker

- To enable the children to get into role, ask the children, in their small groups, to discuss: Who they are/What job they do/How they might use the beach in the photograph/How they spend most of their time/If they are rich or poor/What parts of the beach they might need for work/What parts they might use for pleasure?

- Ask each group to imagine that a hotel is going to be built by the travel company. How does the hotel change things? Will their way of life be affected? Will some changes be for the better? Will some changes be for the worse? Do they want the hotel to be built?

- Ask each group to list three statements which express their views (in role) about this proposed development.

- Ask the children to form six new groups, each comprising representatives from the original groupings.

- Ask the children in the new group to take it in turns (in their original roles) to give views and discuss their statements, to listen to the views of others and to consider whether their view has changed.

- Ask children to return to their original groups and to elect a spokesperson.

- Organise a mock public enquiry and allow each of the representatives to speak for two minutes.

- Ask children to vote 'for' or 'against' the hotel and discuss the idea of 'rated' votes: that the local government and travel company groups' votes are rated at two compared with the votes of the local residents, local child, fisherfolk and holidaymaker (rated at one).

- The weighting provides an opportunity for discussion of who holds the power and why this might be so. In many developing countries some groups, such as women and youths, have virtually no say in their country's development. Discuss with the children whether this is fair and ask children who has the most power in this decision-making process and why.

- A whole-class discussion out of role – consider the following: Do they feel they had a fair say? Who held the power? Why do they think this was?

- How much did their own group's interests affect the decision to build or not to build the hotel? What issues did the groups raise?

- Were some issues common to all groups? What were the greatest differences between groups and why?

- Write an account of the role-play activity in the role of a journalist attending the public meeting.

Figure 4: The Role Play (Adapted from Mason, 1992).

Figure 5: Discussion Genre.

Discussion Genre
What do you think? Should there be a development of a hotel complex and tourist centre in the rainforests of North Queensland?
(Link to *Where the Forest Meets the Sea*, Baker, 1989.)

In *Where the Forest Meets the Sea* there is a lot of discussion about whether it is necessary to have a hotel complex and tourist centre in the rainforests of North Queensland.

The main arguments *for* building a hotel complex and tourist centre in the rainforest are:

■

■

■

On the other hand, there are also strong arguments *against* building a hotel complex and tourist centre in the rainforest:

■

■

■

After looking at the different points of view and the evidence for them,
I think that:

To support my view, I would like to draw attention to the following evidence:

Natural
These are questions about the environment – energy, air, water, soil, living things, and their relationships to each other. These questions are about the 'built-as well as the 'natural' environment.

Who decides
These are questions about power: who makes choices and decides what is to happen, who benefits and loses as a result of these decisions and at what cost?

Economic
These are questions about money, trading, aid and ownership.

Social
These are questions about people: their relationships, traditions and culture, and the way they live. They include questions about how, for example, gender, race, disability, class and age affect social relationships.

Figure 6: The Development Compass Rose. Source: DEC (Birmingham), 1995.

Activities for key stage 1 – Katie Morag and the Isle of Struay

This example is linked to the book called *Katie Morag and the New Pier* by Mairi Hedderwick (1993). It relates to the citizenship and literacy unit (unit 3) in the QCA's scheme of work, QCA/DfEE, 1998. The aim here is to investigate the impact of change on people's lives. As the new pier is built on the Isle of Struay, Katie Morag feels both excited at the prospect of seeing Granny Mainland more often and sad when she realises that her friend the ferryman will lose his livelihood when the large steamer is able to dock in the bay. An unexpected winter storm, however, provides the ferryman and his wife with new ways to make a living. **(citizenship)**

Activities: (citizenship activities)

▪ After reading the book, ask the children (in groups) to discuss who lives on the island and what work they do.

▪ Read the story and look at the pictures on the first and the last two pages of the story. What things are changing on the island? Why? How do you feel about the changes? How do you think the islanders feel about the changes? (Encourage the children to express views about these changes.)

▪ Use a writing frame to put forward the cases for and against the building of the new pier.

▪ In role (e.g. Struay Parish Councillor, islanders, ferryman, UK Travel Company owner, Katie Morag, fisherman, conservationist) debate the issue of the new pier and the changes it will bring. Which children are for the changes and which ones are against?

▪ How will the lives of the islanders be changed with the building of the new pier? Compare and contrast the jobs people did before and after the construction of the pier. Who will be most affected? Who will be better off? Who will be worse off?

▪ Make a tourist map and brochures advertising the island. Include all the information and pictures of what you can see.

▪ List the types of foods that are produced by the farmers and fishers on the island. Write a menu for the ferryman's cafe. Use local food (produce) from the farms and the sea. Give your dishes names appropriate to the island setting. Will the visitors to the island want locally produced food on the menu or will they demand the type of food they are used to at home?

TEACHING STRATEGIES: USING PHOTOGRAPHS

Much work in primary geography involves the use of photographs which is a method of informing and involving children that can help them become aware of issues, both locally and globally (Figure 7).

Figure 7: Using photographs.

Questioning photographs	Mount photograph on large sheet of paper. Children work in small groups or pairs. Children write questions around the mounted photograph. These questions can be exchanged with another group, so children can find answers to each other's questions or the questions can be used for focused research.
Similarities and differences	Look at photographs. Children in groups draw up two lists, one of photographs of children leading similar lives to that of children in UK (own locality), and one that shows children leading very different lives.
Issues	Ask the children to look at a photograph(s) and identify the particular issue(s) (e.g. water, children's rights, education, child labour). Ask the children to discuss in groups how the issue is affecting the people who are in the photograph. Who can the children contact to get further information? Who can give them the knowledge to empower the children to do something about the issue?
Sort into sets	Ask the children to sort photographs into sets according to issues (e.g. water, waste, traffic, child labour).
Venn diagrams	Give the children six photographs of their own and six photographs of a contrasting locality. Ask the children to draw a venn diagram. What issues are typical of the contrasting locality? What issues are typical of own locality? The intersection will contain issues that are the same.
Speech bubbles	Select a picture that features people or a person and an issue. Ask the children to cut out and write in speech bubbles what the people might be saying about the issue and how it is affecting their life and environment.
Brainstorm	Ask the children to brainstorm adjectives about the photograph – may be positive or negative.
Captions	Put the children into groups of three or four. Give each group the same set of photographs (three or four photographs). Ask each group to write captions for each photograph, but give each group a different brief (e.g. to write the caption for a large tour company, a fund-raising organisation, for a government publication, for the planning authority, for an industrialist, for a developer). Display the captions from each group and ask the others to guess what the brief was.
Add a value	Children are asked to add a set of values to the photograph and then discuss (e.g. happy, fun, tired, crowded, rich). The children select and discuss a photograph (which includes an issue) they don't like. They put forward reasons why the issue might have developed, who might have influence, what might be done by themselves, etc.

Look at me	Ask the child to draw a picture of self. Stick on to selected photograph of the other place. Ask child to describe how they feel standing in that environment – what can s/he see, hear, smell? What does s/he like/dislike? Where does s/he think s/he might be? Who might s/he meet there? What animals might live there?
Jigsaw activity 1	Choose photographs of different environments. Give children a photograph with one or two pieces missing. What do they think the missing piece(s) is (are)?
Jigsaw activity 2	Choose photographs of different environments with different issues. Cut into a jigsaw. Exchange one or two pieces. Can the children spot which pieces have been exchanged? – before they complete the jigsaw?– after they have completed the jigsaw?
Guess the picture	Display photographs, around the room for a day or two, of different environments with different issues portrayed. Ask one child to choose one photograph in secret. This child then has to describe it to the other children as if they were standing in the middle of the picture. The other children have to guess which photograph it is and what the issue is.
An exhibition of an issue (locally and globally)	Children select six photographs to use to make an exhibition to show an issue which affects children both locally and globally. Write captions. This could be done in pairs/groups. Hold a class discussion about the issue – who could they contact to get additional information and what can they do to help resolve the problem?
Tell the story	In pairs, children look at a photograph and then undertake one of the following: (1) write a joint description about the issue(s) in the photograph, or (2) one child starts the description and the other writes about the actions which could be taken to solve the problem, or (3) the teacher might like to start the description for the whole class and the children discuss and write about the actions that could be taken to solve the problem.
Time tales	The children discuss what might have happened before the photograph was taken to cause the issue and what might happen after the photograph was taken to help solve the issue.

Professional development activities

1. Study the detail and implications of the citizenship strand of the non-statutory framework for PSHE/citizenship. Consider current schemes of work and determine to what extent they support young people's understanding of the nature and working of democracy and citizenship at all scales. Carry out an audit (ideally in conjunction with all other curriculum areas) which identifies:

■ where citizenship is currently being delivered;

■ what issues need to be considered for implementing citizenship (level of funding and resourcing, training, relationship between school and its partners in the community);

■ where citizenship education activities might be developed in order to enhance geographical education, support progression and/or to cover cross-curricular delivery across the school.

2. Ask staff to carry out a SWOT (strengths, weaknesses, opportunities, threats) analysis as an awareness-raising activity and the first step towards planning for the introduction of citizenship education (the template below should be provided on an A4 piece of paper). This activity will enable colleagues to consider their understanding of the citizenship strand of the non-statutory framework for PSHE/citizenship, and their views about its implications for the delivery of citizenship within the primary geography curriculum.

Strengths of integrating aspects of the non-statutory framework for PSHE/citizenship into the primary geography curriculum	**Weaknesses** of integrating aspects of the non-statutory framework for PSHE/citizenship into the primary geography curriculum
Opportunities presented by integrating aspects of the non-statutory framework for PSHE/citizenship into the primary geography curriculum	**Threats** posed by integrating aspects of the non-statutory framework for PSHE/citizenship into the primary geography curriculum

3. Management issues: discuss how citizenship will be managed within the school.

■ Who will have overview and responsibility?

■ How much time should be allocated?

■ Who will co-ordinate the policy?

■ Does the delivery of citizenship match the aims and ethos of the school?

■ How does citizenship education contribute to school improvement?

■ What arrangements for monitoring, evaluating and reviewing progress are required?

References

Baker, J. (1989) *Where the Forest Meets the Sea.* London: Walker Books.

DEC Birmingham (1995) *Development Compass Rose - A Consultation Pack.* Birmingham: DEC.

Hedderwick, M. (1993) *Katie Morag and the New Pier.* London: Bodley Head.

Mason, P. (1992) *Learn to Travel – Activities on Travel and Tourism for Primary Schools.* Godalming: WWF.

Oxfam (1999) *Put Yourself on the Line: A Teacher's Guide to Global Citizenship.* Oxford: Oxfam.

QCA/DfEE (1998) *A Scheme of Work for Key Stages 1 and 2 Geography.* London: QCA/DfEE.

QCA/DfEE (1999) *The National Curriculum, Handbook for Primary Teachers in England, Key Stages 1 and 2.* London: QCA/DfEE.

QCA/DfEE (2000) *A Scheme of Work for Key Stages 1 and 2 Geography: Update.* London: QCA/DfEE.

Further reading

Development Education Association (1999) *Human Rights Guidance for Key Stages 1 and 2.* DEA.

Hampshire County Council (1998) *Citizenship Education (A Planning Framework for Citizenship in Schools: Guidelines on Policy and Practice)* Hampshire County Council.

MCC/DEP (1998) *Take Part! Speak Out! Education for Citizenship in Primary Schools.* MCC/DEP.

RSPB *Our World - Our Responsibility: Environmental Education - A Practical Guide.* RSPB.

Sustainable Development Education (1998) *Lessons in Life.* SDE.

Symons, G. (1998) *Making it Happen: Agenda 21 and Schools.* Godalming: WWF.

UNICEF *Talking Rights, Taking Responsibilities (Activities for Secondary English and Citizenship).* A UNICEF photopack.

Walkington, H. (1999) *Theory into Practice: Global Citizenship Education.* Sheffield: Geographical Association.

Photo: Steve Pratchett

Personal, social and health education (PSHE)

Chapter 2

Elaine Jackson

What is PSHE?

PSHE is concerned with preparing children for life now and in the future. It is about developing pupils' self-knowledge and their ability to understand and manage their feelings, to handle relationships with other children and adults and to deal with changes in their daily lives. PSHE involves not only the children, but the whole school, their families and the communities in which they live, so strong links between home, school and community are essential. PSHE is about what the children perceive as healthy lifestyles and what they have to do to ensure they live a healthy life.

PSHE needs to start from the children themselves and use their experiences. It has to be relevant to them and encompass their different backgrounds, beliefs and concerns. The aim is to enhance the children's self-esteem and personal effectiveness and to encourage high expectations. To achieve this, it helps to use real-life examples and situations; these motivate children and make them feel that their work has a purpose and goal. For learning to be effective, it must involve communication, collaboration, self-directed learning, problem solving, researching and publishing findings.

There is a strong connection between primary geography – its content, teaching and learning strategies (including fieldwork) – and PSHE. At the core of primary geography is the concept of real people in real places and their relationship with their environment. The primary geography curriculum encourages children to study places at a range of scales, from local to global, and to explore the interdependence of society, economy and the natural environment. Children study how people are influenced by and affect their environments and they are encouraged to develop a sense of responsibility for personal and group actions. Primary geography provides opportunities for learners to encounter and engage in 'live' issues; issues which may cross a range of scales, from local to global, and require active participation and personal responses. Primary geography questions the values on which decisions are based and explores alternative ways of providing for human needs and wants.

Acknowledgement that global equity and justice are essential elements of sustainability and that basic needs must be met universally will have an enormous impact on our future. Primary geography and PSHE can be highly influential in this regard, especially when taught in learning environments which are free from prejudice and discrimination and where children have the desire to participate.

Primary geography and PSHE both involve the application of the six key skills to real issues and concerns. These skills are: communication, working with others, problem solving and learning, information technology, application of number and improving own learning and performance. The involvement of pupils in real-life issues, and the working through of problems and solutions which have an impact on their own lives, helps them understand that their contribution does make a real difference. This ownership and involvement makes the learning more meaningful and exciting and helps children become aware of the wider world and how that world works economically, socially, culturally, technologically and environmentally.

PSHE, taught through primary geography, helps to develop or encourage:

- the development of critical thinking and effective information processing skills
- opportunities for pupil interaction, group activities, co-operative working, collaboration, reasoned debate, negotiation and informed decision making
- an understanding of how the decision-making process works
- an understanding of the place of the individual in society, and of collective rights and responsibilities
- the ability to express opinions, solve problems and communicate with others on a local/national/international basis, including using ICT
- the development of confidence to explore, adapt and shape technological understanding and skills
- creativity – the ability to seek out alternatives
- cultural understanding of other societies
- empathy, and an awareness of the points of view of others
- an understanding that the quality of life is not dependent on standard of living

Recently, the drive for school improvement has centred on curriculum content, curriculum delivery and the inspection process. This has resulted in less emphasis and status being given to areas not directly part of the national curriculum. Also, the pressure for league table success and the introduction of the literacy and numeracy strategies (both based on good practice) have taken precedence over those aspects of the curriculum associated with developing the broad range of skills and knowledge associated with preparation for adult life. PSHE, when linked with primary geography and other national curriculum subjects, develops many of the skills and attitudes that contribute to raising standards, school improvement and high achievement. They also contribute to the quality of the environment and the quality of life for the children after they leave school. The wide range of teaching and learning strategies employed by PSHE underpin the very basis of effective education across the curriculum. Furthermore, it has been shown that involvement of the wider community in education enhances pupils' performance in the whole curriculum.

What are the new requirements?

The new requirements for the delivery of PSHE at key stages 1 and 2 take the form of a flexible, non-statutory framework. This framework is found in *The National Curriculum, Handbook for Primary Teachers in England, Key Stages 1 and 2* (QCA/DfEE, 1999). The framework is designed to build on and extend current good practice, allow different schools with different needs and interests to focus on issues pertinent to their situations, and provide opportunities for all pupils to learn and achieve. The learning framework will enable schools to prepare their pupils for the opportunities, responsibilities and experiences of life through more explicit and coherent provision in the area of PSHE.

" *Personal, social and health education (PSHE) and citizenship help to give pupils the knowledge, skills and understanding they need to lead confident, healthy, independent lives and to become informed, active and responsible citizens. Pupils are encouraged to take part in a wide range of activities and experiences across and beyond the curriculum, contributing fully to the life of their school and communities. In doing so they learn to recognise their own worth, work well with others and become increasingly responsible for their own learning. They reflect on their experiences and understand how they are developing personally and socially, tackling many of the spiritual, moral, social and cultural issues that are part of growing up. They also find out about the main political and social institutions that affect their lives and about their responsibilities, rights and duties as individuals and members of communities. They learn to understand and respect our common humanity, diversity and differences so that they can go on to form the effective, fulfilling relationships that are an essential part of life and learning.' (QCA/DfEE, 1999, p. 136)*

PSHE was designed, not to be a 'free standing' subject, but to introduce a process approach to issues, problems and situations which develops children's skills and confidence, as well as knowledge. In a world of constant change, with the possibility of information overload, how children learn (the process) is as important and may be more important than what (the content) they learn. The national curriculum may dictate what *should* be taught, but not *how*. Adults of the future will need to be flexible, adaptable and co-operative and this involves a wide range of teaching strategies and learning styles. PSHE involves the children in taking their learning beyond the school walls so that they can be effective in the wider world and help to change things for the better; linking elements of PSHE with primary geography provides a relevant and motivating means of helping children to develop the skills they need to achieve this.

Planning issues: ways in which primary geography may support PSHE

This section highlights some of the main ways in which primary geography can contribute to PSHE through its content and its teaching and learning strategies (including fieldwork).

Primary geography can promote:

PERSONAL DEVELOPMENT through the following:
Moral development through considering the consequences of actions and decisions made, through investigating environmental issues (e.g. global warming, balancing people's current needs against the needs of future generations), through exploring issues of right and wrong, values (the standards against which we are judged, self respect, respect for others) and conflicts (human rights, refugees, etc.).
Cultural development through helping children recognise differences and similarities between cultures and within cultures, through studying the local area and environment of the school and considering how this reflects the cultures of the local inhabitants.
Spiritual development through helping children to respond to dramatic environments, both physical and human.

SOCIAL DEVELOPMENT through the teaching and learning strategies adopted (enquiry approach, group work, fieldwork, analysis of data, use of ICT, etc.), and through investigating the impact of development on the quality of life of different groups of people in different countries.

HEALTH EDUCATION by helping children understand that their quality of life depends on their physical, social and mental well-being.

Figure 1 (overleaf): Example of a key stage 2 planning matrix, based on Unit 20 'Local traffic – an environmental issue' in (QCA/DfEE 1998) – with PSHE and citizenship activities added.

Links between the PSHE/citizenship framework are shown in Chapter 1, pages 10-21. Figure 1 (overleaf) shows how PSHE activities can be added to an existing scheme of work.

About the unit: This is a 'long' unit. It deals with a local traffic improvement scheme (a bypass) and the impact it will have on local people and the environment. **The unit has been designed so that it can be adapted easily for any local issue.** The issue could be concerned with other traffic improvement schemes (e.g. speed ramps, one-way streets, cycle lanes, pedestrian crossings, routes for handicapped people) or a quite different issue (e.g. a proposal for quarrying, the effect of a hypermarket on existing shops, the effect of demolishing old houses to create a new site with different potential uses like a leisure centre or mosque, building a BMX track).

The key questions for any issue are likely to be:

What is the issue? – identify it clearly from maps, photographs, local knowledge
Where is the issue? – how far does it extend?
Why is it an issue? – which groups are in favour of this scheme and which against?
What are the views of the different groups involved?
What do the class think about the issue?

ENQUIRY QUESTIONS	LEARNING OBJECTIVES	POSSIBLE TEACHING ACTIVITIES	LEARNING OUTCOMES	POINTS TO NOTE
What are the issues involved in constructing the bypass?	■ about the issues involved in a change in the local environment ■ to locate features on a map ■ to relate maps to photographs ■ to carry out an interview	■ Provide opportunities for the children to identify the key issues about the traffic bypass scheme through looking at maps, newspapers and photographs, and carrying out local surveys and interviews with key people. ■ Visit the site of the bypass. **PSHE activities – safety:** ■ **Group work:** Before the site visit, ask the children to reflect on the environment in which the site visit is taking place through the geographical enquiry questions (Where is this place? What is this place like? etc.). ■ **Whole class:** Brainstorm, discuss and anticipate areas of danger. ■ **Group work:** Ask the children to design their own rules and own codes of practice for the visit. ■ **Whole class:** Discuss emergency First Aid procedure with personnel from St. John's Ambulance. **Group work:** design a First Aid box. ■ **Group work:** List contents of First Aid box. ■ **Group work:** In groups, describe appropriate dress for the weather conditions, terrain, fieldwork activity, etc.	■ understand the nature of the issue	**Speaking and listening:** prepare children for interviewing by encouraging them to discuss the nature of the task and the amount of formality required. Ask them to consider the effect this has on the language they will use. **PSHE activities – Safety** See teaching activities column Teachers must be aware of their responsibilities when taking children out of school to undertake fieldwork. Teachers must undertake Risk Assessments and pre-visits, so that they are aware of the dangers, and must have up-to-date information to ensure personal safety and hygiene rules are followed at all times.
Where is the bypass located?	■ to use maps at a variety of scales ■ to identify key physical and human features ■ how features influence the location of human activities	■ Ask the children to locate the area of road construction using Ordnance Survey maps and relate the development to the main roads, local villages and towns and local land forms (e.g. hills, valleys).	■ understand how human and physical features in the area affect the bypass construction	
Why is the construction of the bypass an issue?	■ about recent or proposed changes in the locality	The main purpose of the activity is to make children aware that they can make important contributions, however small these may appear to be, to environmental problems.	■ summarise and categorise the range of views involved	**PSHE activities** See teaching activities column

ENQUIRY QUESTIONS	LEARNING OBJECTIVES	POSSIBLE TEACHING ACTIVITIES	LEARNING OUTCOMES	POINTS TO NOTE
	■ about a particular issue arising from the way land is used	**PSHE and citizenship activities:** **Whole class:** Brainstorm – What is the issue/problem now? How is the issue expressed (e.g. complaints to newspapers, local protests, meetings, accident statistics, people's own experience). Who will be affected by the proposed bypass? Who wants the bypass? Who does not want the bypass? Who are the stakeholders/Who makes the decisions?		
How did the issue arise?	■ to use secondary evidence to compare before and after	■ Ask the children to investigate how the land was used and what the area was like before construction began. They could use maps, photographs, old newspapers, documents and oral history in their research.	■ identify environmental changes arising from the construction of the bypass	Environmental education: this work links to conflict resolution.
What are the groups involved in the issue and what are their views?	■ how people affect their environment ■ that different people hold different views about an issue	■ With the children's help, devise and carry out a questionnaire survey of the main groups involved.	■ know the views of different people about the issue ■ know who are likely to gain and lose from the issue	**PSHE and citizenship activities:** through these activities children will begin to understand how decisions are made at the local scale.
	■ how and why people seek to manage and sustain their environment	■ Divide the children into small groups and ask each group to analyse the data collected in the questionnaire survey. Ask them to use the results of their analysis to suggest ways the issue might be resolved. They could use ICT to present their suggestions. ■ Explore different ways to improve the traffic problem in the area, by looking at different views about the issue and its resolution. Children are encouraged to engage actively in the issue. Debate an issue (bypass) or better still debate a real 'live' issue within your locality and involve personnel from different groups with interests in the development. ■ **Role play:** Through role play, preconceptions can be challenged and empathy developed by exploring different points of view about environmental, safety and development issues. Ensure, when you develop the role-play cards, that there is a strong emphasis on health and safety issues. ■ **Debate in role** (e.g. parents, children, farmers, commuters, local wildlife trust, local councillors, highways dept., MP. Conduct a role play of a public meeting, concluding by asking groups to decide what they think should happen next. Give the children role cards with the different opinions, ensuring there is a strong emphasis on health and safety issues. Try to reach a concensus. Discuss who the most powerful stakeholders were and why they were powerful.	■ play a role in a simulation of a public meeting ■ suggest ways in which the issue might be resolved ■ express and justify their own views on the issue	

Teaching methods and learning activities

1. Keeping safe (personal safety)

(1a) Residential visits

Children derive a great deal of educational benefit from taking part in residential visits and undergo experiences not available or possible in the classroom. These visits help develop investigative skills and encourage greater independence. Often the foci of these visits are related to geographical studies (fieldwork, a contrasting locality, rivers, settlements, etc.)

Many other skills are developed, including personal and social skills, and skills related to the focused curriculum area(s). The range of experiences enhances the children's self confidence, helps them to work co-operatively and builds team-work skills.

Group work: before the visit, ask the children to reflect on the environment in which the visit is taking place through the geographical enquiry questions (Where is this place? What is this place like? etc.).

Whole class: Brainstorm, discuss and anticipate areas of danger.

Group work: Ask the children to design their own rules and own codes of practice for the visit.

Whole class: Discuss emergency First Aid procedure with personnel from St John's Ambulance and/or Warden of the Centre.

Group work: Design a First Aid box.

Group work: List contents of First Aid box.

Group work: In groups, look at the weather data for the residential centre, think about the time of the year that the visit is taking place, the terrain and the type of fieldwork activities, etc.

either

Develop a kit list for the visit and pack a suitcase

or

Describe appropriate dress for the weather conditions, terrain, fieldwork activity, etc.

(1b) Day visits

COASTAL VISITS

Whole class: Brainstorm, discuss and anticipate areas of danger (e.g. tides and currents/sand banks/warning signs and flags/dangers of paddling and swimming/hazards on beach – glass, barbed wire, sewage outflows/cliffs)

Group work: Write a Code of Practice for the children on the visit or produce a safety poster for visits to the coast.

FARM VISITS

Whole class: Brainstorm, discuss and anticipate areas of danger (e.g. farm machinery, animals, diseases)

Group work: Write a Code of Practice for the children on the visit or produce a safety poster for visits to the farm.

RIVER

Whole class: Discuss National River Authority's water safety rules.

Group work: Design a set of water safety rules for a visit to a river.

Whole class: Each group to present their safety rules to the whole class. Class vote on the best set of safety rules which then become the water safety code for the class.

(1c) Fieldwork in the local area and on visits

Teachers must be aware of their responsibilities when taking children out of school to undertake fieldwork. Risk assessments and pre-visits should be undertaken and up-to-date personal hygiene rules should be studied and followed at all times (e.g. wear plastic gloves when undertaking river studies). Policies for work in the local environment and on day and residential visits must be discussed, understood, adopted and acted upon by all staff and Governors.

(1d) Safety at home and at school

Group work: In turn, give each group a picture of areas at home, at school and in the local area (e.g. kitchen, playground, garden, roads, railway lines) where the children might encounter dangers. The children discuss the dangers and highlight how each scene in the picture could be made safer. They then produce a map of each area, showing how it can be made safer.

(1e) Development of a playground

Whole class: Discuss what might make a playground unsafe (vandalised play equipment, dog mess, strangers, drug dealers and users, etc.). Discuss ways of making the playground a safe environment. Design and map out the development of the school grounds, ensuring the views of the people affected have been taken into account.

(1f) Safe routes to school

Traffic issues have an impact on everyone and at all scales – local, regional, national or global. Issues of safety, pollution, health, management of scarce resources and sustainability can all be considered in the context of a survey of traffic, and studies of how places are connected and how people move between those places.

Group work: Ask the children to write a questionnaire to find out how most children travel to school (use ICT if appropriate, e.g. *Junior Pin Point*). Ask the children to carry out the questionnaire survey and then to analyse the resulting responses (use ICT to help).

Individual work: Ask each child to mark his/her route to and from school on a map of the local area. (Younger children can draw simple pictorial maps instead of using the local area maps.) Ask each child to conduct a safety audit (risk assessment) of the route and means of travel they use. Can they identify danger spots (e.g. junctions, corners, parked cars), hazards (cracked pavements, potholes, bad parking, speeding) etc.? Are there any hazards that affect a particular group of people (disabled, elderly, people with push chairs)? Ask each child to mark with an 'X' all the places where they have to cross a road.

Group work: In groups, ask the children to look at each other's routes to school and the danger points. Ask the children how the dangers could be reduced.

Group work: Ask the children to plan a safe walking route to include safer crossing places (pelican and zebra crossings, bridges, islands, school crossing patrol points, etc.) and measures to reduce traffic speed (speed humps, speed restrictions, etc.). Ask your local Road Safety Officer to come to school to work with the children (e.g. practical pedestrian training schemes). Ask the children to contact their local councillors and show them the safe route, explaining to them about the danger spots. If the children feel it is appropriate, they could ask the councillors to act on their findings.

*2. **Wants and needs*** (an activity which could be used when studying a less economically developed country at KS2)

The purpose of the activity is to develop the children's understanding of the differences between 'wants' and 'needs' and 'quality of life' and 'standard of living'.

Whole class: Brainstorm what children think they need to lead a happy, healthy life.

Work in pairs: Ask the children to choose nine items from the brainstorm and rank them according to which they feel are most important. They can use the diamond ranking system with the most important at the top, the least important at the bottom and the others in between.

Group work: (three sets of pairs): Compare lists and discuss. Each group to repeat the exercise to make a combined group list.

Group work: Ask the children to put the words into two columns – WANTS and NEEDS.

Ask the children to underline the five things which they consider to be most important for their happiness.

Group work: Give each group a different photograph of children's lives in the EDC they are studying. Ask each group to apply the geographical enquiry questions to their photograph. Repeat the same exercise on WANTS and NEEDS for the children in the group's photograph.

Whole class: Discuss each group's response.

Group work: Ask the children to reflect on what they really need to be happy and healthy and to have a good quality of life. Ask the children to revise their original lists of wants and needs. Do they want to move some items from one list to another?

Whole class: Have a class discussion about the meaning of 'quality of life' (friends, open spaces, pure air, etc.) and 'standard of living' (bigger house, better car, etc.).

Group work: Ask the children, in their groups, to produce a poster illustrating 'quality of life'.

Whole class: Explore with the children who is responsible for our quality of life and reflect on how increasing our standard of living could have an impact on the environment and other people's lives, both now and in the future.

3. Games from round the world (see UNICEF Games for Summer Playtimes)

One of the Articles of the UN Convention on the Rights of the Child is the right of children to play. Games around the world helps children explore play in different countries and cultures as well as involving co-operation and participation.

4. Role play and circle time

Circle time involves the whole class and is often used as an introduction to a topic or issue to find out what the children already know or what their attitudes are to that issue. Circle time may also be used to review what the children have learnt or how attitudes have been influenced by their work.

Seating arrangements in circle time are mixed and it is good practice to start with a non-threatening issue then move gradually to more serious ones. During circle time everyone has the opportunity to be listened to and to put forward their point of view. Circle time helps develop skills of discussion, and encourages both independent learning and learning though co-operation.

(4a) Achievement and success

Activities focusing the children's attention on personal achievements. Obstacles can affect their progress and eventual success, but obstacles can be overcome either by personal or group effort.

Role play: The teacher asks children to imagine they are going on a journey. They must act out what happens and try to imagine how they feel as they travel. The teacher provides them with all kinds of terrain, obstacles and difficulties to overcome (e.g. cross a sticky, muddy swamp in a tropical rainforest, climb a steep mountain, cross a wide river)

After many obstacles and difficulties they reach their destination and celebrate.

Circle Time: Ask children how they felt when they were on the journey and when they reached their destination. The children are prompted to acknowledge that success is a good feeling. Relate these feelings to their own lives and school work.

(4b) Taking responsibility for own behaviour, thereby enhancing achievement

Role play: Children are given an imaginary task set in a geographical context (e.g. booking a holiday, packing the suitcases and travelling to go to a certain destination). The children have to decide where they want to visit and find out something about that place, the type of clothes they will need and how they are going to get there. Each child in the group is instructed to take on a role and to behave in a certain way all the time (e.g. sulky, bossy, lazy, bad tempered, nasty) The children are asked to explore, through role play, what would happen if they set about their given task as a group, but behaved in their allotted manner.

Circle Time: The teacher asks if they were able to complete their task. Was it difficult? If so why? The children are guided through discussion to realise and acknowledge that certain aspects of their behaviour could affect their own and other people's achievements.

Circle Time: Pass round the 'magic microphone' and ask the children to complete the sentence: I could do better if ... (e.g. I didn't sulk, I wasn't grumpy, I tried to be kinder).

(4c) Causes and effects of problems – opportunity for children to recognise when a problem exists and to find workable solutions to problems.

Group work: Each group (of four children) is given a jigsaw depicting something of geographical relevance (e.g. physical features, buildings round the world, different environments and habitats, houses round the world). In each group, one piece of the jigsaw has been swapped with a piece from another group's puzzle. After a short time the teacher asks how the groups are getting on. When it is clear to the children that they cannot complete their puzzles, the teacher asks what is wrong. Once the groups realise what the problem is, the teacher asks each group to hold up the piece that does not fit so that the other groups can find their missing piece and complete their jigsaws.

(4di) Co-operation – to learn skills needed to co-operate with others (social skills).

Group work: In groups of four or five, the children are told they are working in a factory on a production line. Each group has to decide on a product to make and every member of the group has to have a task in making the product, each of which must be mimed. In their groups, the children are given time to decide on their product and practice their mime. The groups take it in turns to perform their pieces. The audience are told what the end product is. Then the children perform their actions again, but this time they actually say what they are doing.

(4dii) Personal effectiveness – production of Induction Booklet.

Year 6 children in primary school are asked to produce the new Induction Booklet for the High School. This gives the children an increased sense of ownership, team membership, etc. The book should include maps and plans of the High School and a description of how to get there. Bus timetables, information about bus passes and car parks, etc., should be included.

Professional development activities

1. Study the detail and implications of the non-statutory framework for PSHE (QCA/DfEE, 1999). Consider current schemes of work for primary geography (and other subjects) and determine to what extent they support children's understanding of PSHE. Carry out an audit (ideally in conjunction with all other curriculum areas) which identifies:

    ■ where PSHE is currently being delivered;

    ■ where there are other opportunities to promote PSHE;

    ■ where PSHE activities might be developed in order to enhance geographical education, support progression and/or to cover cross-curricular delivery throughout the school.

2. Ask the staff to carry out a SWOT (strengths, weaknesses, opportunities, threat) analysis as an awareness-raising activity and the first step towards planning for the delivery of PSHE through geography (the template below should be provided on an A4 piece of paper). Review current practice to identify success and opportunities for further work. This activity will enable colleagues to consider their understanding of the non-statutory framework for PSHE and their views about its implications for delivery within the primary geography curriculum and other curriculum areas.

Strengths of integrating aspects of the non-statutory framework for PSHE into the primary geography curriculum	**Weaknesses** of integrating aspects of the non-statutory framework for PSHE into the primary geography curriculum
Opportunities presented by integrating aspects of the non-statutory framework for PSHE into the primary geography curriculum	**Threats** posed by integrating aspects of the non-statutory framework for PSHE into the primary geography curriculum

3. Discuss how successful implementation of PSHE will:

    ■ contribute significantly to the future lifestyle of every child and prepare them for life beyond school;

    ■ help develop and consolidate home-school and school-community relationships;

    ■ contribute to a healthy school ethos;

    ■ raise standards by motivating children and helping them enjoy school;

    ■ help bring the school's mission statement to life;

    ■ contribute to success in Ofsted inspections.

References

QCA/DfEE (1999) *The National Curriculum, Handbook for Primary Teachers in England, Key Stages 1 and 2*. London: QCA/DfEE.

QCA/DfEE (2000) *A Scheme of Work for Key Stages 1 and 2 Geography: Update*. London: QCA/DfEE.

UNICEF *Games for Summer Playtimes*. UNICEF leaflet.

Environmental change and sustainable development

3

Chapter 3

Maggie Smith
Alan Reid

What is environmental change and sustainable development education?

Environmental change and sustainable development education overlap considerably with environmental education. Environmental education in turn has strong links to the geography subject area. Geography is a subject with one of the biggest responsibilities for delivering the knowledge, understanding and skills that enable young people to develop an appreciation of environmental issues. The subject's distinctive enquiry approach, the opportunities it gives for the development of skills such as problem solving and decision making, and the opportunities afforded for first-hand study of the environment, can help develop awareness of the nature of physical and human environments, and the complexity of inter-relationships between them. Thus, children can begin to explore the implications of people's (including their own) values, attitudes and actions. These links are clearly seen in all the aims of geography as set out in the position statement issued by the Geographical Association:

> ■ *'To develop in young people a knowledge and understanding of where they live, of other people and places, and of how people and places interrelate and interconnect; of the significance of location; of human and physical environments; of people-environment relationships; and of the causes and consequences of change.*
>
> ■ *To develop the skills necessary to carry out geographical study, e.g. geographical enquiry, mapwork and fieldwork.*
>
> ■ *To stimulate an interest in and encourage an appreciation of the world around us.*
>
> ■ *To develop an informed concern for the world around us, and an ability and willingness to take positive action both locally and globally.' (GA, 1999, p. 1)*

In 1996, SCAA published *Teaching Environmental Matters through the National Curriculum* in which the links between environmental education and the specific requirements of the existing (1995) national curriculum at all key stages were set out, and examples of good practice given. This review of the links between the statutory subject areas and environmental education showed geography to be a primary vehicle for environmental education at key stages 1 and 2, along with science and (to a lesser extent) art and PE. The 1995 revision of the national curriculum had introduced a specific environment-based thematic study into geography at each key stage, for example 'The quality of the environment' at key stage 1 and 'Environmental change' at key stage 2. This replaced the attainment target called 'Environmental geography' which operated across all key stages in the original (1991) version of the national curriculum. In the latest version of the curriculum, the environmental aspect of geography remains much as before, thus ensuring that geography continues to be an important vehicle for teaching and learning about the environment.

'Environmental education is the process of recognising values and clarifying concepts in order to develop skills and attitudes necessary to understand and appreciate the inter-relatedness among man, his culture and his biophysical surroundings [sic]. Environmental education also entails practice in decision making and self-formulation of a code of behaviour about issues concerning environmental quality.' World Conservation Union (IUCN, 1970)

Objectives for environmental education, as set out in the Belgrade Charter:

1. To foster clear awareness of and concern about economic, social, political and ecological interdependence in urban and rural areas.

2. To provide every person with opportunities to acquire knowledge, values, attitudes, commitment and skills to protect and improve the environment.

3. To create new patterns of behaviour of individuals, groups and society as a whole towards the environment. (UNESCO, 1976)

A liberal interpretation of the prepositional model of environmental education, based on the Tbilisi recommendations (Palmer, 1998):

■ education *about* the environment (that is, basic knowledge and understanding of the environment and human interactions, through studying the local or wider environment);

■ education *in* or *through* the environment (that is, using the environment as a resource for learning, especially skills and competencies, with an emphasis on enquiry and investigation and pupils' first-hand experiences); and

■ education *for* the environment (nurturing caring values, attitudes and positive action for the environment, through personal responsibility and empathy).

A socially critical interpretation of the prepositional model of environmental education (Fien, 1993):

'Education *about* the environment is the most common form of environmental education. Its objectives emphasise knowledge about natural systems and processes and the ecological, economic and political factors that influence decisions about how people use the environment.

Education *through* the environment uses pupils' experiences in the environment as a medium for education. The aims of this learner-centred approach to environmental education are to give learning reality, relevance and practical experience and to provide pupils with an appreciation of the environment through direct contact with it...it may also foster environmental concern if pupils become captivated by the importance and fragility of ecosystems...or immersed in the values conflict over an environmental issue.

Education *for* the environment has an overt agenda of values education and social change. It aims to engage pupils in the exploration and resolution of environmental issues in order to...promote lifestyle changes that are compatible with the sustainable and equitable use of resources. In doing so it builds on education about and through the environment to help develop an informed concern for the environment, a sensitive environmental ethic, and the skills for participating in environmental protection and improvement.'

Figure 1: Aims and objectives in environmental learning.

'Education is critical for promoting sustainable development and improving the capacity of the people to address environment and development issues...It is critical for achieving environmental and ethical awareness, values and attitudes, skills and behaviour consistent with sustainable development and for effective public participation in decision making.'
(UNCED, 1992)

Definitions

Two definitions of education for sustainable development are offered by the Sustainable Development Education Panel (SDEP, 1999:30). The first is aimed at policy makers:

'Education for sustainable development is about the learning needed to maintain and improve our quality of life and the quality of life of generations to come. It is about equipping individuals, communities, groups, businesses and government to live and act sustainably; as well as giving them an understanding of the environmental, social and economic issues involved. It is about preparing for the world in which we will live in the next century, and making sure that we are not found wanting'.

The second is aimed at the schools sector:

'Education for sustainable development enables people to develop the knowledge, values and skills to participate in decisions about the way we do things individually and collectively, both locally and globally, that will improve the quality of life now without damaging the planet for the future.'

Key Concepts of Sustainable Development

'Sustainable development concerns a wide range of interrelated issues which may be approached through the following seven principles or dimensions. The first concerns the interdependent nature of the world. This gives rise to the need for a participative response through the exercise of citizenship and stewardship, which is the theme of the second concept.

"The third through to sixth concepts cover further key dimensions of sustainable development, leading to the seventh which, as a logical consequence of those that precede, is concerned with the limits of knowledge and exercise of the precautionary principle.

1. Interdependence – of society, economy and the natural environment, from local to global
2. Citizenship and stewardship – rights and responsibilities, participation, and co-operation
3. Needs and rights of future generations
4. Diversity – cultural, social, economic and biological
5. Quality of life, equity and justice
6. Sustainable change – development and carrying capacity
7. Uncertainty, and precaution in action.'

The principles are exemplified with guidance statements in the Sustainable Development Education Panel First Annual Report, 1998. General learning outcomes and specific learning outcomes at each key stage associated with the seven key concepts are also listed there, and at:
http://www.environment.detr.gov.uk/sustainable/educpanel/1998ar/ann4.htm

Figure 2: Education for sustainable development.

Sustainable development education combines elements of environmental education with development education. This reflects recent broader shifts in thinking about the environment; the key ideas have been shifting away from being exclusively connected with the natural environment to embrace urban environments and 'artificial' environments, and to stress sustainability and its relation to moral, cultural, spiritual, economic and political considerations (Huckle and Sterling, 1996; Palmer, 1998).

Figures 1 and 2 (pages 46 and 47) show some definitions and concepts relating to environmental education and education for sustainable development.

What are the new requirements?

Curriculum 2000 (QCA/DfEE, 2000) has, as one of its 'broad set of common values and purposes', a commitment to valuing '...the environment in which we live'.

This was the message from David Blunkett and William Stubbs in the jointly signed Foreword to the version of the national curriculum published in 1999.

Encouraging news indeed for those who have an interest in furthering the awareness of environmental learning in primary education; but how does this overarching commitment to valuing the environment translate into practical teaching requirements for the individual subject areas of the curriculum, and how far does a study of environmental change and sustainable development go towards the fostering of those values?

In the new curriculum, study of environmental concerns has not only held its place within the programmes of study for geography, but has an enhanced role (Figure 3). The thematic studies have gone but 'Environmental change and sustainable development' is now one of the three key elements of knowledge and understanding for geography, sitting alongside knowledge and understanding of places, and of patterns and processes. These three elements, together with geographical enquiry and skills, make up the content of the geography programmes of study.

	1995 Order Thematic study	Curriculum 2000 Knowledge and understanding of environmental change and sustainable development
Key stage 1	6. The quality of the environment Pupils should be taught: ■ to express views on the attractive and unattractive features of the environment ■ how that environment is changing ■ how the quality of that environment can be sustained and improved	5. Pupils should be taught to: ■ recognise changes in the environment ■ recognise how the environment can be sustained and improved
Key stage 2	10. Environmental change Pupils should be taught: ■ how people affect the environment ■ how and why people seek to manage and sustain their environment	5. Pupils should be taught to: ■ recognise how people can improve the environment or damage it, and how decisions about places affect the future quality of people's lives ■ recognise how and why people may seek to manage environments sustainably, and to identify opportunities for their own involvement

Figure 3: Curriculum changes in geography.

Thus, there is very little change at key stage 1. Most of the detail of the thematic study 'Quality of the environment' is now found in the 'Environmental change and sustainable development' element. The one statement that is missing (the requirement for children to express their views on attractive and unattractive features of the environment) has been moved to geographical enquiry (see below). At key stage 2, however, there are some welcome advances. The first is that children will be looking at decision making and its implications for the first time in primary education – an important part of understanding how situations come about and a key element in looking at ways forward. Second, the term 'quality of life' is introduced at key stage 2 and it is clear that we will need to look at ways to teach this concept to younger children. Third is the requirement that we enable children to identify opportunities for their own involvement in sustainable management of environments – a significant move towards recognising the importance of young people making a personal response to the issues raised and actively participating in working towards solutions.

Another change within the geography programmes of study is the higher profile for geographical enquiry – now the vehicle through which geographical skills are developed. Geographical enquiry and skills together make up the fourth key element of the geography programmes of study. The 'geographical enquiry and skills' element contains two requirements that relate in a particularly important way to the study of the environment. The first is the requirement at key stage 1 for children to be taught to develop their own views about people, places and environments. Similarly at key stage 2 it is encouraging to see a requirement that children should be taught to 'identify and explain different views that people, including themselves, hold about topical geographical issues'. Obvious candidates for the topical issues are (at a variety of scales) those to do with environmental change and sustainable development, including planning issues, resource use, and pollution issues.

The other key change to the programmes of study for geography is the addition of a section called 'breadth of study', which sets out the contexts through which knowledge, understanding and skills should be delivered. At key stage 2, children must now study an environmental issue (specifically an issue caused by environmental change) and attempts to manage the environment sustainably (e.g. traffic congestion, drought and hedgerow loss). Thus, they now have an opportunity to investigate issues in which they can get actively involved.

For geography, therefore, there is an enhanced role for the study of environmental change and sustainable development. Perhaps this is reflected in the fact that the geography statement of 'importance' is the only subject statement to address the environment and sustainable development directly:

> 'Geography is a focus within the curriculum for understanding and resolving issues about the environment and sustainable development.' (QCA/DfEE, 1999, p. 108)

For geographers, the important task now is to grasp these opportunities and develop them into a substantial and central area of geographical teaching and learning.

Geography has by its nature a distinctive contribution to make to environmental responsibility and sustainable development. However, the nature of the causes and effects of, and solutions to, environmental issues means that study of them must range across subject boundaries. So how have other subjects changed in terms of their role in delivering environmental education and education for sustainable development in Curriculum 2000?

The answer is that the requirement to consider the environment still remains in many subject areas of the new curriculum. There are still substantial contributions to environmental understanding in science, design and technology, and art. The wording of some subject areas suggests a higher profile than before for environmental considerations (for example in art and in design and technology); and the inclusion of citizenship and PSHE in the curriculum provides many important opportunities for introducing and developing ideas and concepts linked to the environment and sustainability.

Thus, although still confined within the knowledge, understanding and skills section of the programmes of study for the individual subject areas of the national curriculum, the teaching of the concepts of environmental awareness and of sustainable development is now firmly established in the new curriculum.

Ways in which primary geography may support environmental change and sustainable development education

DEVELOPING AN HOLISTIC APPROACH

It is questionable whether environmental awareness and awareness of sustainability can be confined within the subject areas of the formal curriculum. An appreciation of environmental change and the concept of sustainability involves not only knowledge, understanding and skills but also the consideration by children of their values and attitudes – of their behaviour and lifestyles and of the lifestyles and behaviour of others – and the impact of that behaviour on the environment. It needs to be set within a social context. Research has shown that knowledge alone does not necessarily inform behaviour, or as Slater (1994) put it: 'Giving pupils the facts and leaving them to make up their own minds doesn't work.' The school community as a whole needs to have a common philosophy and ethos of caring for the environment and for the promotion of sustainability. This sets a model of good practice in front of the children and means that the ethos permeates throughout the school.

A necessary condition for this approach to work is that the staff and head teacher must uniformly understand and engage with all aspects of the philosophy. The school's approach to estate and resource management will be affected and there might be budgeting considerations. The school may need to reach out into the local community and open up links.

A starting point used in many schools is to build environmental responsibility and sustainability into the school's aims. Consider the following, as examples:

Aims of the school
- To develop an awareness of living as a caring member of the wider community with a positive role to play.
- To develop a joy of learning itself, supported by well-developed skills for continuing independent learning in our technological society.
- To develop an appreciation and exploration of each individual's resourcefulness set against a background of humanity's creative achievement, and create a caring, stimulating and stable environment, developing a happy working partnership between home, community and school.
- To develop an understanding and appreciation of the environment and the importance of sustainability.

Our mission statement
It is our aim to develop moral and spiritual awareness, including respect and understanding, in a happy caring environment.

MAKING USE OF LOCAL AGENDA 21

The following text is adapted from an article by Bullard (1998) in the *Journal of Geography in Higher Education.*

In 1992, 178 countries attending the United Nations Conference on Environment and Development (UNCED: the Rio 'Earth Summit') signed Agenda 21. Agenda 21 is a non-binding treaty that sets out a framework of political recommendations designed to protect the environment and move towards sustainable development. One chapter of the Agenda is devoted to educational issues in the broader sense. It is here that specific mention of the role of education in promoting Agenda 21 is made. Section 36.5 recognises that, to be effective, environmental and development education should be included in all disciplines at all levels of education.

Bullard (1998) describes an activity for undergraduates where seminar discussions and Internet resources are used to stimulate debate and enhance pupils' understanding of Local Agenda 21 as part of a series of learning activities on resource management. Emphasis is placed on exploring local authorities' Local Agenda 21 strategies and examining how these are being implemented and monitored. This technique can be adapted to key stage 3 schemes of work that seek to investigate the methods and motives for local environmental management, and the ways in which global-scale policy decisions are filtered down to the level of the individual. The following enquiry questions might be used to structure the learning, with teachers and pupils working in conjunction with Local Agenda 21 officers to investigate local solutions to wider problems:

- Which aspects of sustainability are highlighted in Local Agenda 21 action plans?
- To what extent is your local authority's strategy a 'wish list'?
- Exactly how is sustainability going to be achieved?
- How will the effects of the Local Agenda 21 strategy be monitored?
- How is public participation in Local Agenda 21 being encouraged?
- On which environmental resources does the Local Agenda 21 strategy focus? Why do you think this might be?

As suggested by Bullard, teachers, pupils and the wider community might also ask:

- What do you consider to be the role of the school in Local Agenda 21? How is the school and its members already involved?
- How do the actions and proposals in the Local Agenda 21 strategies relate to other geographical themes in your schemes of work?
- Is Local Agenda 21 likely to be an effective route to environmental management in the school and community?

The exercise can make extensive use of the Internet to provide high volume information from a diversity of sources and at low cost to the institution. Bullard's case studies use links to Tagish's *Directory of UK Local Authority websites* and the UK Government's list of organisations which list all UK local authority websites. Web addresses for these are, respectively:

http://www.tagish.co.uk/tagish/links/localgov.htm
http://www.open.gov.uk/index/filclgov.htm

The full text of Agenda 21 is available from a number of sources including a United Nations supported website at: gopher://gopher.un.org:70/11/conf/unced/English

In general, the most detailed information is available by county councils and city councils rather than borough councils, with very comprehensive coverage of LA21 strategies from:

Surrey County Council: http://www.surreycc.gov.uk/scc/environment/country.html
Cheshire County Council: http://www.cheshire.gov.uk: 80/cheshpln/la21/eb.htm
Newcastle-upon-Tyne City Council: http://www.newcastle-city-council.gov.uk/ag21b.htm

PLANNING THE CURRICULUM

Another issue that merits discussion is that of planning the curriculum for effective environmental awareness. Several questions that you might think about are suggested below:

- How will children be given opportunities to consider decision making and its effects on the environment?

- How will children be given opportunities for their own involvement? What kind of involvement will that be? How can children's involvement be directed towards positive action for a better and more sustainable environment?

- The new requirements remain largely concerned with the development of the cognitive dimension connected with environmental awareness. Is there scope within the curriculum to open up the affective domain – is an exploration of children's emotions and feelings built in to schemes of work?

- Is the need to challenge children's misconceptions and misunderstandings built in to the schemes of work? Are children guided towards being able to reflect critically on and examine popular conceptions of environmental issues and sustainability?

- How is continuity and progression across the two key stages ensured? How can continuity and progression from key stage 2 to 3 be effected? How can your teaching be part of children's lifelong progression in understanding about environmental change and sustainability?

Careful and creative planning will be needed to ensure that children have a balanced curriculum of environmental learning, and new approaches to teaching and learning may need to be developed.

Teaching methods and learning activities

While undoubtedly the content of any curriculum for environmental education and education for sustainable development is important, perhaps what is just as vital is the way in which the body of concepts and skills is taught in geography. The issues to be covered can be sensitive and controversial, and the uncertainty which surrounds them can sometimes prove unsettling for younger children. What is needed, therefore, is a secure and fitting teaching and learning setting within which children can explore and develop their own understanding, skills and values in ways which best equip them personally to become caring and actively involved citizens.

There are many strategies that teachers will already be experienced in using that help to build this confidence in young children. Activities such as group work, learning through stories, play and drama, and circle time – amongst many others – are equally appropriate for teaching about environmental issues and sustainability as they would be for any other topic, and should be selected to suit the varied needs of the pupils being taught, and the constraints of the physical and human working environment of the school.

However, as primary teachers who are geography specialists, or have the role of geography co-ordinator, are already aware, geography can offer distinctive approaches that are particularly well suited to the teaching of environmental change and sustainable development. Teaching and learning strategies such as enquiry-based learning, decision making, fieldwork and making and using maps are now well established in the teaching of geography at all levels and would lend themselves particularly well to studies of environmental change and sustainable development (see list of suggested reading at the end of this chapter which includes some of the publications in which these learning styles are described in more detail).

What follows here is an exploration of two aspects of experiential learning – through fieldwork and through place studies.

1. Fieldwork

Fieldwork, as used here, means activities that take place outside the classroom, e.g. in other parts of the school buildings, the school grounds, the local area – be it urban or more natural – or a more distant location visited for a day or part of a day. Fieldwork enables children to 'connect with' the environment by providing the opportunity for them to study it at first hand.

'Traditional' teacher-led fieldwork, as in a guided walk around the local area or an investigation in the school grounds, is familiar to teachers and has its place. However, there are other styles of fieldwork that may not be quite so well known and that open up different possibilities for children to explore their ideas about environmental change and sustainability.

Discovery fieldwork encourages children to identify features in a landscape that seem important from their point of view and which are interesting to them, rather than following a pre-determined routine set out according to the interest of the teacher. By deciding what should be the focus of their own studies, children are taking control of their own learning and high levels of motivation and interest can be generated. There is of course the risk that the topics then chosen are not part of the curriculum as desired by the teacher.

Sensory fieldwork, as the name suggests, encourages children to engage their senses and emotions in relation to the environment. Children can think about colours, sounds and textures and link their feelings to creative expression, e.g. art, language and music. Children may then be encouraged to think what it is that makes a place unique (and so start to develop a sense of place), about things that have or are changing in that environment, and how they feel about that environment. As Job *et al.* (1999, p. 17) argue, if we are to develop a caring and responsible approach to the environment in our future citizens, then 'engagement of senses and emotions may be as important as the application of rational and analytical thinking'.

Of course the fieldwork approaches described above need not necessarily be developed in isolation. Job *et al.* (1999) set out a model that shows how a number of fieldwork strategies, including those above, can work in an integrated way (see Figure 4 overleaf).

2. Place studies

A consideration of the environment – how it is changing and how it can be managed sustainably – starts in many schools with an exploration of the local environment. Concepts, skills and values that are developed in a local and familiar setting can then be transferred and developed when studying more distant locations and environments. Some children find it difficult to imagine or to empathise with landscapes, climates, patterns of life and daily situations of which they have no direct personal experience.

Ashley (1999:208) demonstrates this in a description of children's reactions to the notion of restricted access to fresh water that applies in many part of the developing world. He points out that children who had only experienced life in the UK, where fresh water is readily available for drinking, cooking, bathing, washing the car, and so on, would find it difficult to appreciate a situation where water is not available on demand. There are many excellent resource packs which can be used to try to get over this 'experience' problem. Packs such as *Focus on Castries St Lucia*

Figure 4: Integrated
fieldwork strategies.

Awareness/Acclimatisation	**Strategy**
Activities to heighten awareness based on personal experience of an environment, involving sharpening of perceptions, development of critical visual analysis and communicating personal responses.	Using sensory and discovery strategies
Learners discover their own route into the environment by finding a personal point of contact.	
Investigation	
Participants identify a focus for further investigation then carry out individual or group enquiry to further knowledge and understanding.	Enquiry-based investigation
Concern/action	
Development of feelings of personal responsibility for an environment and a desire to participate in decisions which affect it.	Personal decision making Application

(Bunce *et al.*, 1997) use photographs and suggest role plays to familiarise children with unfamiliar environments and lifestyles.

An alternative, or indeed a complementary, approach is to use personal contact between children in the two locations. The personal contact can be set up through known links such as parents or friends (one classroom teacher used one of her own friends, conveniently also a teacher, who was working overseas), or through links developed in the community, such as twinned towns, or through organisations that make educational links like this available to schools (e.g. the Central Bureau, see end of chapter). The links can take the form of letters (sent by post, by fax or by e-mail), tape or video recordings, or pictorial displays (so bringing in links with literacy, communication, using ICT, etc.). Children can be encouraged to ask questions of the children in their partner school that enable them to visualise and understand more easily lifestyles and environments that are different from their own. This might lead to an exploration of what is meant by 'quality of life', and might well stimulate children to think about positive actions and changes in lifestyle that they can make in order to bring about change and promote sustainability.

Other activities

Activities like the following help children to think about what the environment will be like in the future.

Whole class: Brainstorm – What is the issue/problem now? (e.g. development of school grounds, Eco-schools, Agenda 21). The main purpose of the activity is to make children aware that they can make important contributions, however small these may appear to be, to environmental problems.

The issues children raise mainly fall into four categories (all of which create a link between primary geography, PSHE and citizenship).

Categories	Problems
■ Pollution	■ litter and dog dirt – health hazards
	■ exhaust fumes – health problems
	■ CFCs – chlorofluorocarbons, aerosol sprays, destroying ozone layer, cancer
■ Conservation of energy	■ use of exhaustible fossil fuels (coal, oil, gas)
	■ excessive burning of fossil fuels – acid rain, greenhouse effect, global warming
	■ use of nuclear fuels
	■ wasting energy in the home
■ Waste	■ disposable society
	■ use of plastics and material which is no longer biodegradable
	■ unhealthy and unsightly disposal of plastics
■ Protection of wildlife and nature	■ destruction of woodlands and rainforests
	■ destruction of animal habitats

Whole class: Discuss what is likely to happen in 5, 10, 15 years time
What would the pupils like to happen?
If the future is to be different, what needs to change?

In groups: Ask the children to discuss and list the actions they could take to help ensure the future quality of the Earth and the health and safety of the people who live there. Overleaf are some ideas children have come up with.

Aims, outcomes and assessment

Whatever the teaching and learning activities used to deliver education about environmental change and sustainability, it is essential to consider first what your educational goals are. To ensure continuity and progression it is obviously best if this is taken as a whole-school decision. One whole-school approach to determining environmental and sustainability goals is shown in Figure 5.

One of the biggest challenges involved in teaching about environmental change and sustainable development is assessing it. The assessment of children's knowledge,

Actions children could take (environmental issues)
- Switch off light when room not in use
- Pick up litter
- Make sure your dog doesn't mess where children play and people walk
- Recycle glass and use recycled paper
- Reuse milk bottles and carrier bags
- Take old clothes, toys, etc., to charity shops
- Recycle paper/newspapers (including shredding)
- Use both sides of paper, save envelopes and stamps
- Don't leave taps running when brushing teeth, and put plug in sink
- Take a shower instead of a bath
- Use 'green' (ozone friendly) cleaning products
- Buy things loose rather than pre-packaged
- Cycle or walk rather than use a car
- Conservation of energy – home insulation of lofts, walls, tanks, windows, etc.
- Protecting wildlife, woodlands and rainforests

understanding and skills may well be relatively straightforward and can use existing methods of formal and informal assessment, formative and summative assessment with which teachers are familiar. But how can you measure children's values; how can you assess the changes that they might make in their behaviour and lifestyles; and how can you assess positive action that children might take in order to promote sustainability? One thing that you can do, though, is to assess their ability to use the knowledge and understanding they have gained.

Professional development activities

1. Look at Figures 1 and 2 on pages 46-47.
   a) Which ideas and approaches are you familiar with?
   b) Do any of these ideas and approaches form part of your teaching?
   c) For those that are part of your present teaching, what are their strengths and weaknesses?
   d) What might we assume that pupils already know or can do before we begin teaching about environmental change and sustainable development? What would you intend that they should know or be able to do after you have finished? Is a shared school view on this necessary?
   e) What knowledge of subject content, teaching and learning styles and resources is required for the preparation of teaching about environmental change and sustainable development?
   f) What interests and stimulates you personally, and as a teacher, about environmental change and sustainable development?

2. How far can awareness of the environment and of sustainability contribute to *all* the aims of the school? To what extent might there be conflict between the aims?

3. Do you include fieldwork in your teaching of work connected with the environment and sustainability? What style of fieldwork do you use? Can you see advantages in incorporating different styles of fieldwork (including those above) into your teaching in the future?

Knowledge

As a basis for making informed judgements about the environment, pupils should develop knowledge and understanding of:

- The natural processes which take place in the environment
- The impact of human activities on the environment
- Environmental issues such as pollution
- How human lives and livelihoods are dependent on the environment
- How the environment is affected by decisions and actions
- The importance of planning, design and aesthetic considerations
- The importance of effective action to protect and manage the environment
- The interdependence of individuals, groups, communities and nations

Skills

To develop a range of skills through first-hand experiences. In particular, develop communication skills through discussion, debate, and negotiation.

- Numeracy skills
- Problem-solving skills
- Personal and social skills
- Study skills
- Information and technology skills
- Research and data handling
- Critical thinking
- Creativity

Attitudes and values

Promoting positive attitudes towards the environment is essential if pupils are to value it and understand their role in safeguarding it for the future. The development of attitudes and personal qualities as listed below will contribute to this process:

- A commitment to the well-being of all living things
- A desire for social justice
- Empathy and awareness of the points of view of others
- An understanding that quality of life is not just dependent on standard of living
- An understanding of the place of individual and collective rights and responsibilities
- A belief that through working with others they can make a difference
- A belief in a positive future

Figure 5: Education for sustainability: objectives

References

Ashley, M. (ed) (1999) *Improving Teaching and Learning in the Humanities*. London: Falmer Press.

Bunce, I., Foley, J. and Morgan, W. (1997) *Focus on Castries, St Lucia*. Sheffield: GA.

Bullard, J.E. (1998) 'Raising awareness of Local Agenda 21: the use of Internet resources', *Journal of Geography in Higher Education*, 22, 2, pp. 201-210.

CE (Council of Europe) (1988) *Council and the Ministers of Education Meeting within the Council: Resolution on Environmental Education*. (88/C177/03) Strasbourg: CE .

Fien, J. (1993) *Environmental Education: A Pathway to Sustainability*. Geelong: Deakin University Press.

GA (the Geographical Association) (1999) *Geography in the Curriculum: A Position Statement.* Sheffield: GA.

Huckle, J. and Sterling, S. (eds) (1996) *Education for Sustainability.* London: Earthscan.

Job, D, Day, C. and Smyth, T. (1999) *Beyond the Bikesheds.* Sheffield: GA.

Munton, R. and Collins, K. (1990) 'Government strategies for sustainable development', *Geography*, 83, 4, pp. 346-357.

Palmer, J. (1998) *Environmental Education in the 21st Century: Theory, Practice, Progress and Promise.* London: Routledge.

QCA/DfEE (1999) *The National Curriculum, Handbook for Primary Teachers in England, Key Stages 1 and 2.* London: QCA/DfEE.

QCA/DfEE (2000) *A Scheme of Work for Key Stages 1 and 2 Geography: Update.* London: QCA/DfEE.

SCAA (1996) *Teaching Environmental Matters through the National Curriculum.* London: SCAA.

SDEP (Sustainable Development Education Panel) (1999) *First Annual Report 1998.* London: DETR.

Slater, F. (1994) 'Education through geography: knowledge, understanding, values and culture', *Geography*, 79, 2, pp. 147-163.

UNCED (1992) *UN Conference on Environment and Development: Agenda 21 Rio Declaration.* Paris: UNESCO.

UNESCO (1976) The Belgrade Charter, *Connect*, 1, 1, pp. 1-3.

Further reading

Carter, R. (ed) (1998) *Handbook of Primary Geography.* Sheffield: Geographical Association. This invaluable handbook provides information on teaching styles that are pertinent to the teaching of environmental change and sustainable development, and has an excellent reading list.

For more detailed information on the teaching of environmental change and sustainable development the following may be helpful:

Ashley, M. (ed) (1999) *Improving Teaching and Learning in the Humanities.* London: Falmer Press.

Chambers, B. *et al.* (1995) *Awareness into Action. Environmental Education in the Primary Curriculum.* Sheffield: Geographical Association.

Neal, P.D. and Palmer, J. (1990) *Environmental Education in the Primary School.* Oxford: Blackwell.

For more information on the fieldwork strategies described above:

Job, D., Day, C. and Smyth, T. (1999) *Beyond the Bikesheds.* Sheffield: Geographical Association. (Note: This book is aimed at KS3 and above but many of the ideas can be used as they stand or be adapted to KS1 and 2.)

For more information on making links as described above:

Beddis, R. and Mares, C. (1988) *School Links International: A New Approach to Primary School Linking around the World.* Tidy Britain Group/WWF.